Walls

Stones always tell us long stories. They are natural formations that reflect the growth and decay that occurs over the course of time. Man senses something unique in stone that helps him express his thoughts. In this way we find our connection to the tried and true and our unison with nature.

In stones we find gravity and lightness, nature and elegance, beauty and simplicity. Among the other features of stone structures is the deep need for perfection, which manifests itself in the high demands of the designer and his disciplined mode of expression. Stones connect the time-honored to the new.

Werner Blaser, Basel, 2003

Günter Mader and Elke Zimmermann

Walls

Elements of Garden
and Landscape Architecture

W. W. Norton & Company

New York • London

Translation by Anna Steegmann

Technical consultation: Florian Oberhuber

Mauern, Elemente der Garten- und Landschaftsarchitektur by Günter Mader,
Elke Zimmermann Copyright © 2008 by Deutsche Verlags-Anstalt, Munich,
a division of Verlagsgruppe Random House, Munich, Germany
English translation copyright © 2011 by W. W. Norton & Company, Inc.

For information about permission to reproduce selections from this book, write to
Permissions, W. W. Norton & Company, Inc., 500 Fifth Avenue, New York, NY 10110

For information about special discounts for bulk purchases, please contact
W. W. Norton Special Sales at specialsales@wwnorton.com or 800-233-4830

Manufacturing by KHL Printing Co. Pte Ltd
Production manager: Leeann Graham
Electronic production: J. Lops

Library of Congress Cataloging-in-Publication Data

Mader, Günter.
  [Mauern. English]
Walls : elements of garden and landscape architecture / Günter Mader, Elke Zimmermann.
     p. cm.
  Includes bibliographical references and index.
  Translation of: Mauern : Elemente der Garten-und Landschaftsarchitektur.
  ISBN 978-0-393-73294-8 (pbk.)
  1. Walls. 2. Garden structures. I. Zimmermann, Elke. II. Title.
  TH4965.M3313 2011
  717—dc22
                         2010031110

W. W. Norton & Company, Inc.,
500 Fifth Avenue, New York, N.Y. 10110
www.wwnorton.com

W. W. Norton & Company Ltd.,
Castle House, 75/76 Wells Street, London W1T 3QT

0 9 8 7 6 5 4 3 2 1

Contents

6 **Foreword**

8 **The cultural history of wall construction**

12 Town walls
14 Waterside walls
14 Garden walls
14 Walls in the cultural landscape
14 *Terraced walls*
16 *Field walls*
18 Fortified national borders
18 *The Great Wall of China*
20 *The walls of the Roman Empire*
20 *The Berlin Wall*
20 *The wall between Israel
   and Palestine*

22 **Design fundamentals**

24 Structural fundamentals
24 *The foundation*
26 *The base*
26 *Masonry*
28 *Coping*
32 *Expansion joints*
32 Planning basics
32 *Height*
34 *Thickness*
34 *Walls on a slope*
34 *Legal concerns*

36 **Stone masonry walls**

40 Dry-placed walls
46 Dry-placed walls of split blocks
48 Dry-placed walls of boulders
   and river stones
50 Rubble stone masonry walls
50 *Coursed masonry*
52 Mixed masonry

54 Walls in the Edwardian style
56 The Stuttgart School
58 The stone masonry walls of
   Ian Hamilton Finlay and
   Andy Goldsworthy
64 Walls of stone masonry palisades
66 Walls of crust slabs
68 Walls with stone masonry cladding
68 *Cemetery walls in Chur
   and Munich-Riem*
70 *The Stuttgart IGA walls*
72 *Kunsthalle Würth in Schwäbisch Hall*

76 **Concrete walls**

78 *Surface design*
82 *Three-dimensional design*
82 *Structural advantages*
82 *The crown*
84 L-shaped precast concrete walls

86 **Clinker brick walls**

88 *Clinker dimensions and wall size*
90 *Jointing*
90 *Wall base and coping*
94 *Clinker walls in landscape planning*
98 Exposed masonry of sand-lime brick

100 **Plastered walls**

102 *Base and finishing coat*
102 *Base*
104 *Crown*
104 *Causes of cracking*

106 **Walls with facings**

108 Steel
110 Glass
110 Wood
112 Plants
112 Hedges

114 **Gabions**

116 *Filling*
116 *Advantages and disadvantages*
118 Design of exposed surfaces
118 Applications
118 Planted gabions

122 **Rammed earth walls**

124 Earth as a building material
124 Garden walls of rammed earth
126 Construction details

128 **Walls of recycled and
    similar materials**

130 Brickworks Park
132 Walls of firewood and other materials

134 **Standards for walls**

135 **Further reading**

135 **Credits**

136 **Photo Credits**

Foreword

Walls are basic elements of garden and landscape design. They define borders, create spaces, and shield a site from view as well as from wind. As retaining walls, they make the design of the topography possible. The carefully enclosed garden surrounded by walls is an archetypal image, and we find it as an ideal concept in all epochs since the beginning of civilization.

Today, many projects in garden and landscape architecture require the design and execution of walls. The reason for a wall may be the technical necessity of managing elevation changes or design factors in creating a space. The enormous variety of walls stems from the materials used and the type of construction as well as from different notions of style, and, last but not least, economic factors. As a rule, walls are one of the most expensive but, at the same time, long-lasting elements of garden and landscape architecture. For this reason they deserve heightened attention during planning and execution.

This book presents numerous design possibilities for walls and open spaces. It is organized by type of construction, material, and method of execution. You will find examples from traditional dry walls typical in some regions and cultures to actual works of land art, from low brick garden walls to elaborate cemetery walls to purely functional noise-barrier walls.

We have applied a clearly structured typology to the systematic gathering of an enormous number of examples, which has enabled us to create a comprehensive design guide. We aim to help raise a new awareness of the design potential of walls in garden and landscape architecture, to inspire and provide you with models and criteria for quality.

While working on our first book, *Fences and Gates,* we became aware that walls are a closely related, fundamental, but nevertheless completely different subject. *Walls* is the logical continuation of our work. The comprehensive picture archive we gathered during our travels challenged us to make a systematic review. We thank Andrea Bartelt-Gering from Deutsche Verlags-Anstalt Munich for her approval of the project and Carla Freudenreich for editing the German edition. We thank Iris von Hoesslin for her attentive layout design.

Günter Mader
Elke Zimmermann

Lycée du Pic Saint-Loup in Saint-Clément-de-Rivière,
Département Hérault, France. This school near Montpellier
was finished in 2008. It shows the extraordinarily successful interplay of austere minimalist structures and walls
of stone masonry. The walls are in charming contrast to
the architecture and fit beautifully into the surrounding
landscape.

Limestone walls and olive tree terraces shape the landscape in Provence, France.

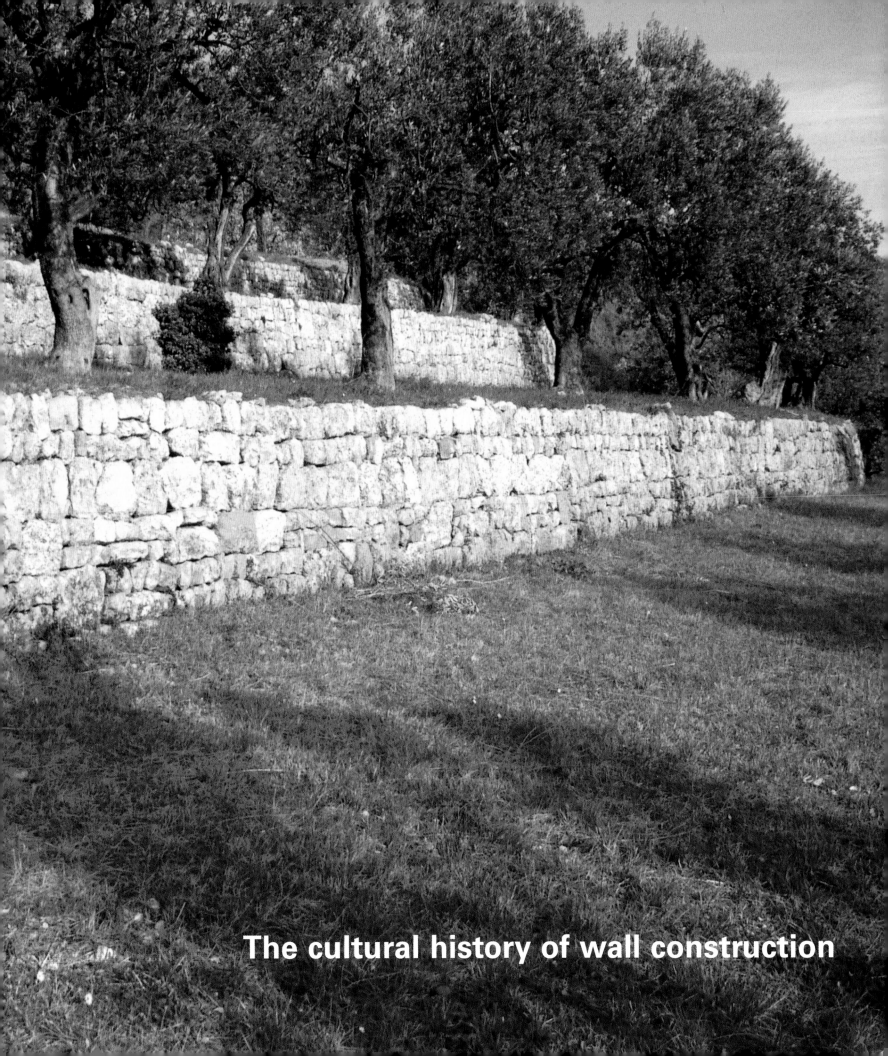

The cultural history of wall construction

The cultural history of wall construction

Cultural history and building history are intrinsically related. Walls are the most important and often the only extant witnesses of building history—they might be relics uncovered at an archaeological excavation site in the Middle East, the cyclopean walls of an Inca settlement in Peru, or the engineered brick masonry walls with decorative borders found in the historic industrial sites of Central Europe.

Our focus will not be on walls connected with buildings but rather on walls as independent elements of a landscape. As such, they are present everywhere in the cultural landscape, in urban development and in garden and landscape architecture as well. Here too their cultural history goes back as far as the history of walls in architecture.

The term *wall* is often carries negative associations, even though it is a basic human need to set boundaries and to protect one's living space with walls. It is important to find the right balance between protection and constriction. Too many boundaries and walls can be pathological in human relationships, in society, or between neighboring countries. A person who is locked in and "walled off" does not participate in the dynamic process of life. A country that isolates and separates itself from the developments in neighboring countries risks its political survival.

With terracing, the inhabitants of Cinque Terre in northern La Spezia have created fertile areas for cultivation from the bluffs. Liguria, Italy.

Through hundreds of years of cultivation and the construction of countless terraces, a unique and characteristic landscape was formed. Colca Valley, Peru.

Machu Picchu, the monumental town ruin of the Incas, is characterized by numerous terraced walls. Near Cuzco, Peru.

This gigantic cyclopean wall from Incan times is still in very good condition and of impressive height; its neatly stacked stones rise as high as 30 feet (9.14 m). Sacsayhuamán, a fortress ruin near Cuzco, Peru.

Town walls

Since the beginning of urban development—starting at the same time as our civilization and cultural history, around 5000 BCE, until the end of the seventeenth century—town walls have been essential and basic to all town settlements. Towns were clearly defined, enclosed, and therefore protected living spaces. The walls that enclosed towns opened only at town gates, thus allowing for a high degree of control. These walls were built, depending on local circumstances and technical possibilities, from boulders or quarry stones, bricks, rammed earth, wooden palisades, or a mix of these construction methods. They guaranteed the safety of the community; because they were used for defense, they were of the utmost solidity. Often they were not just simple town walls, but included battlement parapets, crenellations, embrasures, and towers.

A great number of historical town walls can be found worldwide. They are often of great architectural beauty and of the finest craftsmanship. We can visualize the town walls of Troy, Jerusalem, and Marrakesh, and in Europe many towns still have well-preserved town walls and fortifications. Think of the town walls of Avignon, Avila, Dubrovnik, and Gerona, and the almost completely preserved town walls of Amberg, Dinkelsbühl, Feuchtwangen, Görlitz, Ingoldstadt, Nördlingen, and Rothenburg/Tauber in Germany. In all these cases, the walls are a memorable and dominant element enclosing the historical center of the town.

By the sixteenth and seventeenth centuries simple town walls no longer offered sufficient protection, so elaborate fortifications were built. These consisted of massive ramparts, advanced bastions, moats, and an open front end, the glacis. Matthäus Merian's seventeenth-century engravings of city plans clearly show that all large European cities had such fortifications. Especially impressive examples are in the German cities of Mannheim, Frankfurt, Augsburg, Ulm, and Regensburg.

During the eighteenth century, these fortifications lost their military function, and all over Europe they began to be used as promenades. The ramparts of many German cities were planted with trees, as in Braunschweig, Celle, Erfurt, Hamburg, Hannover, Leipzig, and Lübeck. According to contemporary sources, these transformations were motivated by a desire to beautify the town and by the thought of creating landscapes in civic life. An especially beautiful example, still completely preserved today, is the town wall that the town of Lucca in northern Tuscany made into a promenade planted with large trees.

Paris took a completely different approach. Here, at the end of the seventeenth century, the fortifications were broken apart and remodeled into *grands boulevards* (the word *boulevard* originally meant *bulwark*) with wide circular roads, or parkways, lined with trees. Following the example of Paris, many other European cities completely removed their fortifications. The open spaces thus created were made into parks. The moats became swan ponds. Today, open spaces in the style of English landscape gardens still define many German cities, such as Münster, Bremen, and Lübeck. An outstanding example of a large-scale modeling is Vienna's Ringstrasse, dedicated in 1865. This tree-lined avenue linking a succession of parks spans 2.5 miles (3.23 km) of Vienna's inner city.

In many smaller European cities the medieval town walls were preserved. There was less pressure to remove them because the demolition procedures were too costly. During the nineteenth and twentieth centuries, these historical relics were thought of as monuments worthy of preservation and as an important means of creating identity. They were given landmark status and the towns tried to preserve them as historical monuments, which often involved extensive restoration.

The traditions of urban development include town walls created as fortifications and as boundaries and zoning structures within the town. In all cities it is common to use high walls to separate certain social institutions from the life around them: temples, monasteries, schools, universities, hospitals, barracks, prisons, large manufacturing sites, and churchyards and cemeteries. Walls define clearly marked spaces that have their own rules and regulations, and they help to maintain calm and order within those spaces.

Top right: Town wall of Gerona, Catalonia. Cypresses planted close to the wall create fine vertical contrasts.

Bottom right: This completely preserved town wall, with trees and open space, defines the panorama of Lucca, Tuscany, today.

Waterside walls

Settlements near riverbanks, lakes, or oceans have to be protected from flooding. In coastal flood areas and swampy meadows, new land for urban development and agricultural use was created by extensive construction. Rivers and creeks were straightened and fortified, swamps were drained, and safe ports were constructed. Since ancient times these works and the achievements of their engineers have been celebrated as great progress. Waterside walls protect from the forces of nature, help secure sanitary conditions in cities, and make life easier. Only toward the end of the twentieth century did we recognize the limitations of such development as well as the boomerang effect of massive construction on our complex ecosystems. Then, in some places, people undid or altered these measures. Channelized, drained, or paved waterways were renaturalized. Areas that once served as flood plains were—as far as possible—restored or replaced by naturalistic flood plains to lessen the danger of flooding in other areas.

Many European cities have solidly built waterside walls: along the banks of the Tiber in Rome, the banks of the Thames in London, the banks of the Rhône and Saône in Lyon, and the canals of Venice and those in the historical centers of Dutch towns. Especially beautiful are the banks of the Seine in Paris—enclosed by powerful quay walls and lined by long rows of trees. The waterfront, 2.5 miles (4 km) long, between Pont Sully and Pont d'Iéna, was added to the list of UNESCO's World Cultural Heritage sites in 1992.

In Berlin, after the fall of the Wall, many inner-city areas, including their riverside walls, were restored and developed into prestigious promenades. The banks of the Spree, especially near the government district, have been redesigned with great care to create extensive promenades in the middle of a metropolis. The banks of Berlin-Spandau's Schifffahrtskanal (Shipping Canal) were restored in the 1990s. Public access was provided to a green corridor 5 miles (8 km) long. Today, the quay walls are thoroughly restored and outfitted with solid, well-designed protection devices.

Garden walls

Until the seventeenth century, not only many cities but also many gardens were enclosed by walls. For thousands of years, *garden* meant a separate, enclosed, and protected space. Etymologically, the English word *town*, the Dutch word *tuin* (garden), and the German word *Zaun* (fence) are all related. We find something comparable in Slavic languages, where the root of the word *garden* changes to the endings *-grad, -gard,* and *-gorod* for towns. The meaning is always *enclosure.* Town and garden, as areas of human culture, were both originally removed and protected from the surrounding environment.

Walls protect gardens from uninvited intruders; they define borders and they provide protection from wind and shield the enclosure from view, turning the garden into a habitat with its own rules. An image of the archetypal *hortus conclusus* is still found today in many cloisters and cloister gardens, notably in Great Britain. The kitchen, fruit tree, and shrub gardens there are often designed as walled gardens.

In many places walls are necessary to protect from the wind. They create the microclimate necessary for plants to flourish. These walls are cloaked with espaliered fruit trees, rambler roses, and other climbing plants. The warmth emitted from wall stones is extraordinarily beneficial for growth. Enclosing specific garden areas with walls is an important way of separating and creating spaces within an integrated garden concept.

Walls in the cultural landscape

Terraced walls
Since ancient time humans have appropriated and cultivated land, thereby causing massive changes to the landscape. Flat areas are the easiest to cultivate and irrigate, but often the natural topography leaves much to be desired. Therefore we take charge and redesign the landscape. Thus, in the course of millennia, in many cultures, terraced landscapes were created—for example, the rice fields of the Far East and the cornfields of the fertile valleys of Central and South America. The basic principle of terracing is the same everywhere.

In the European landscape too, especially around the Mediterranean, terrace culture is widespread. Terraces were used for

Above: The shore walls of Berlin-Spandau's Schifffahrtskanal in Berlin-Mitte were restored a few years ago as part of the green corridor project.

Left: The impressive embankment of the Seine with its trees and engineered quay walls characterizes large parts of the cityscape of Paris.

grapevines and olive trees, and for the cultivation of other fruit and vegetables. The gradual leveling of steep slopes is an age-old tradition. In the sunny river valleys of Central Europe, distinctive terrace cultures emerged for viniculture. A technically advanced way of constructing walls was developed that is still characteristic of the region today. Examples are the vineyard terraces in the valleys of the Danube, Mosel, Neckar, and Rhine, and the slopes of Lake Geneva. Terracing makes the cultivation and watering of flat areas easier and protects against erosion. Depending on the kind of cultivation, in certain types of weather the partly exposed soil on slopes might erode down to the valleys, and the valuable layer of humus would be lost. This erosion can be prevented by creating mostly flat areas with the help of walls. The laboriously built terrace walls need constant maintenance if they are to continue to fulfill their purpose. When terraces are no longer cultivated and walls no longer maintained, deterioration and ultimately irreversible erosion damage takes place.

Field walls

In many European landscapes, especially in England, Ireland, and Scotland, but also on the Greek Islands, the Balearic Islands, and other areas in the Mediterranean, we find *dry-placed* (meaning without mortar) stacked fieldstone walls as characteristic elements of the cultural landscape. The landscape was covered with a network of enclosing walls in places where sheep farming traditionally played an important role and where, because of location or the overuse of resources, no lumber for fences was

available. These walls were built either from boulders or from quarry stones found at the site. As long as the old field walls fulfill their function of fencing in grazing land, they are still maintained today and have not been replaced by electric fences. In Great Britain volunteer conservationists often restore field walls; farmers are encouraged by subsidies to care for these traditional dry-placed stone walls.

Dry-placed walls that provide protection from the wind—instead of the hedges found elsewhere—were built where conditions for growing hedges were poor because of the lack of topsoil. These walls could be constructed from boulders found in nearby fields.

Dry-placed walls from Crete to the Scottish Orkney Islands resemble each other in many details. They go back millennia and are often considered prehistoric relics. This points to a common heritage with roots in megalithic culture, as well as to manifold connections during Roman times. But certainly it is also the result of similar basic conditions and technical necessities during construction. In England, the most beautiful

and impressive landscapes shaped by field walls are found in the Yorkshire dales, in the counties of Yorkshire and Cumbria, and in the Cotswold hills, situated mainly in Gloucestershire in England.

Remarkable exceptions are the characteristic field walls on Lanzarote, one of the Canary Islands. Lanzarote was settled in ancient times. It is often suggested that the island is the mythical Garden of the Hesperidins described by Herodotus in the fifth century BCE. Maps and chronicles of the fifteenth and sixteenth centuries document the great fertility of the island. But the eruption of the Timanfaya volcano in 1730 changed the nature of the land completely. The vegetation and cultivated areas were covered with a layer of volcanic ash 3 feet (1 m) thick. In the first part of the twentieth century government programs were designed to help agriculture, and a remarkable way of cultivating the earth was created. Bowl-like plant areas, called *arenados*, were dug out so deeply that they hit the formerly cultivated areas. In the main direction of the wind, small protecting walls—most often laid out in a semicircle—

Top right: Dry-placed walls of the Birsay Cemetery, Orkney Mainland, Orkney Islands, Scotland

Center right: Field walls in the wine-producing region of La Geria, Lanzarote, were considered a work of art by the Museum of Modern Art, New York, in 1960.

Bottom right: In many parts of Great Britain grazing lands are enclosed by dry-placed walls made of stone masonry. Malham, North Yorkshire.

Below: Vineyard terraces on the steep slopes of the Neckar Valley, Germany.

were built from volcanic rock around these dells. A favorable microclimate developed, as condensation water that collects inside the layer of the volcanic ash, chiefly as a result of nightly cooling, quickly moves down through the porous ash and nourishes the roots of the plants. In the middle and northern part of Lanzarote, about twenty thousand acres of land are planned and cultivated in this way. Melons, tomatoes, pumpkins, yams, chickpeas, and onions are grown in the concave plant areas. Fig, peach, and almond trees thrive here also, but the arenados are most important for growing grapes for wine.

Fortified national borders

Throughout history we see that not only cities but also larger political systems and states were searching for a way to create effective boundaries. If countries could not depend on their island location or their hard-to-cross rivers, they had to build fortified borders—fences and walls that functioned as a means of military and economic protection and control. These walls had openings for through traffic and merchandise, which enabled countries and towns to collect taxes and customs duties.

The Great Wall of China

The Great Wall of China, sometimes called the Stone Dragon, is a linear series of walls that was begun 2,500 years ago. It is the most powerful defensive fortification ever built and the longest structure on earth. The first wall-like border fortifications date from the second half of the fifth century BCE and were built by feuding Chinese ethnic groups. In the third century BCE the first Chinese emperor built extensive fortification walls to protect his empire from the Mongols who sought to force their way in from the north. Since then, the wall has been extended and rebuilt again and again; its current shape was created primarily between the fifteenth and seventeenth centuries CE.

Most sections are 10 to 26 feet (3–8 m) high and 20 to 26 feet (6–8 m) wide at the base, decreasing in width toward the top. Depending on local availability, cut stone masonry, burnt brick, or rammed earth was used to construct the exposed surfaces, while the inside was filled with bulk material. The wall served as an arterial road; riders could move quickly and easily on the paved coping that was up to 20 feet (6 m) wide.

Left: The Great Wall of China, the longest structure on earth.

Right: Restored remains of Hadrian's Wall near the Roman fortress of Vercovicium, near Homesteads in Northumberland, in northern England.

The walls of the Roman Empire
Between the first and fourth centuries CE the Roman Empire expanded from the Iberian peninsula to Palestine and from North Africa to the middle of England. It was threatened by enemy countries at its borders. Where there were no natural borders, such as the 1,553 miles (2,467 km) of the Danube River, the Romans were forced to build fortification walls. These were not only useful as a defense against the "barbarians"; they also made it possible to collect customs duty.

In the second century CE the emperor Hadrian built Hadrian's Wall, the northernmost fortification wall of the Roman Empire. Today it remains the most important Roman monument in Great Britain. The wall, outfitted with forts, watchtowers, and eighty gates, was 13 to 16 feet (4–5 m) high and 10 feet (3 m) wide; it spanned 75 miles (120 km) across England, about from what is now the city of Carlisle in the west to Newcastle upon Tyne in the east. About one-third of the original length of the wall is still partly preserved, and it is accompanied by a charming hiking trail. In 1987 it was designated a UNESCO World Heritage site.

In the second and third centuries, the Limes, a border fortification that extended for 340 miles (550 km), was erected in the Roman provinces of Germania Superior and Raetia. Partly a wall, it followed a mysterious, often crooked path from the Rhine to the Danube, from today's Rheinbrohl in Rhineland-Palatine to Regensburg in Bavaria. Archaeologists have shown that the Limes was equipped with nearly nine hundred watchtowers. Each tower was within sight of the next, and messages could be transmitted by beacon-light or horn. The various sections of the Limes that are still preserved are found in today's Hesse, Baden-Württemberg, and Bavaria. They were added to the list of UNESCO's World Heritage sites in 2005.

The Limes Orientalis or Limes Arabicus, which extended for 930 miles (1,500 km) through what is now Jordan and Syria, built between the first and third centuries, was the easternmost defense line of the Roman Empire. It protected the wealthy provinces of Syria and Arabia from the desert nations of the Arabian Peninsula and the troops of the Parthian Empire, the area of today's Iran and Iraq.

The Berlin Wall
To prevent widespread emigration to the Federal Republic of Germany, the German Democratic Republic built the Berlin Wall in 1961. The wall became the symbol of a divided Germany. It had an overall length of 96 miles (155 km), 26.5 miles (43 km) between East and West Berlin, and 69.5 miles (112 km) between West Berlin and neighboring areas of the GDR.

Changes in world politics led to the fall of the Berlin Wall in the autumn of 1989. Several small sections, relics of the original, stand to this day. The East Side Gallery, with its proud slogan "International Memorial for Freedom," is described in travel guides as "the most extensive open-air gallery in the world." This 0.5-mile (1-km) wall segment is the longest continuous part of the Berlin Wall still standing. Located on Mühlenstrasse in the Friedrichshain district, it runs parallel to the Spree River. Soon after the fall of the wall, young graffiti artists from all over the world painted the prefabricated concrete wall segments, creating a distinctive work of art that was declared a historic monument some years ago.

The memorial Berlin Wall at Bernauer Strasse opened in 1998. A complete section of the border zone has been framed between two gigantic steel plates. Here individual portions of the original wall are intact. Visitors can gain insight into the history of divided Germany in the nearby information center.

The wall between Israel and Palestine
During the summer of 2002 Israel was attacked nearly every week by Palestinian suicide bombers. The Israeli government decided to build a border fortification. It was supposed to be 497 miles (800 km) long; 373 miles (600 km) had been completed as of this writing. Near the larger Palestinian cities of Ramallah and Bethlehem it is made of a prefabricated concrete wall 26 feet (8 m) high. Another section is an electronically secured fence with a border strip 197 feet (60 m) wide, outfitted with infrared cameras and motion detectors. It is patrolled by military guards at all times.

The East Side Gallery, proudly named "International Memorial for Freedom," is called the longest open-air gallery in the world. At half a mile long, it is the longest continuous relic of the Berlin Wall. It is located on Mühlenstrasse in the district of Friedrichshain, and it runs parallel to the Spree River. Shortly after the fall of Communism in Germany, the prefabricated concrete wall sections were painted by international graffiti artists. Thus a distinctive work of art was created. It has been declared a historic monument and was given landmark status.

Feldmauer in Ayrshire, Scotland

Design fundamentals

Design fundamentals

Structural fundamentals

We distinguish between *freestanding* and *retaining* walls—a fundamental criterion for differentiating walls. Freestanding walls are used to create boundaries and spaces, while retaining walls are used primarily to stabilize changes in elevation. Freestanding walls must be constructed so they can withstand *wind pressure*; retaining walls have to absorb *earth pressure*.

Walls are structures that have to be carefully planned and executed to comply with local and national building codes and regulations. In Europe they must meet the applicable DIN standards. (Deutsches Institut für Normung, or German Institute for Standardization); equivalent standards in the United States are ASTM (American Society for Testing and Materials) and ANSI (American National Standards Institute). The construction materials used must be finished to the designer's specifications and guidelines. The wall's structural stability must be guaranteed; this means that construction and workmanship have to be consistent with the design criteria.

In traditional wall construction, the wall elements are aligned vertically. They are the foundation, base, masonry, and coping. The following sections describe these elements and their structural features in detail.

The foundation

Wall construction may be *rigid* or *dynamic*. Rigid structures are based on a frostproof concrete foundation of C 20/25 (old name B 25) grade quality (approximately 3190 psi). In most areas of Central Europe, a foundation 32 inches (80 cm) deep is considered frostproof. In a dynamic construction, the foundation is placed directly on the compacted subsoil, or on a frost inhibitor of packed crushed stone, which breaks capillary suction. *Dry-placed walls*, meaning stone masonry created without mortar, are always dynamic constructions, while manufactured masonry, terracotta masonry, or finished limestone are always rigid constructions. Dry-placed stone walls are either based on *foundation stones*— very large and heavy stones that are almost entirely sunk into the soil—set on gravel, or on a strip of lean concrete of C 8/10 (old name B10) grade quality (approximately 1450 psi).

The foundation of a freestanding wall must be able to absorb the forces of the wall's dead weight. The lateral wind forces are transferred by dead weight, by regularly placed thicker piers, and, if necessary, by *cross bracing* in the form of projecting ribs or elbows. The foundation of a retaining wall, on the other hand, must not only absorb the load of its dead weight but also the shear forces resulting from the earth's pressure. Freestanding walls of up to 8 feet (2.5 m) in height and retaining walls of up to 5 feet (1.5 m) in height are standard structures that can be handled by any qualified designer. For higher walls the use of a structural engineer is recommended and often required to obtain the necessary permits and guarantee a structurally sound design of the wall and its foundation.

We distinguish between *linear footings* and *spot footings*. Walls usually bear on linear footings, meaning continuous running linear foundations. Only in special cases are spot footings done; for example in the form of *pile foundations*. These foundations are spanned with *concrete grade beams* and function as the wall's base. This type of construction is occasionally used for cemetery walls, which are especially prone to settling because deep excavation for burials takes place right next to the wall.

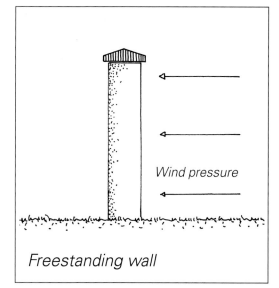

Wind pressure

Freestanding wall

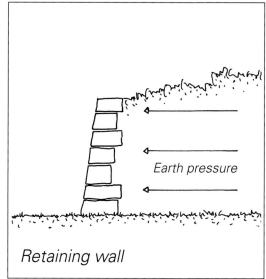

Earth pressure

Retaining wall

Above left: Typical corner treatment with large cut stones, Old Town, Passau, Germany.

Above right: Outdoor spaces at the Lycée du Pic Saint-Loup in Saint-Clément-de-Rivière, near Montpellier, France. The interplay of bold minimalist structures and lively stone masonry is very successful.

Below right: A wall of rough-hewn sandstone. The coping was made from the same material, but with sawn and sandblasted surfaces, giving the wall a solid finish. Oppenweiler, Rems-Murr, Germany.

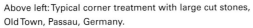

One purpose of a foundation is to distribute pressure, and a foundation with a wider mass safeguards against tilting. A wall that is 9 to 14 inches (24–36 cm) wide usually has a foundation that is 24 inches (60 cm) wide. To make use of the load resulting from the soil's weight, supporting walls are outfitted with an *L-shaped foundation,* whose profile is angled; the foundation connects only to the soil that is retained by the supporting wall. With freestanding walls, the foundation normally abuts equally in both directions as long as the property lines don't make an L-shaped foundation necessary.

The base

A base for walls in open spaces is needed only in special cases—for example, clinker brick walls or finished plastered walls. Constructed of exposed concrete or with a special finish for the lower wall strip, the base should be at least 8 inches (20 cm) above the adjacent cover or reach ground level. The base protects the lower courses of the wall from the impact of splash water and the dirt it carries. The base is clearly different from the wall's main body. It structures the overall appearance and visually reduces the wall's height. In some historic brick masonry designs, the base is called the water table, and extends one course wider than the main structure of the wall; specially manufactured bricks with curved profiles are used to face the wall.

The construction of a base is advisable under certain circumstances for walls of exposed concrete. For example, if there is likely to be soiling in the base area—say from the exhaust fumes of cars that back up toward the wall—a base offers the possibility of partial surface treatment or cleaning. Inlaying a batten into the masonry creates a fine division line and allows the base to be treated differently from the rest of the wall if necessary.

Masonry

If the wall is not constructed with large monolithic blocks or poured concrete but is to be built with stones, we need to secure a stable *masonry bond.* This depends on two factors: the size of the wall and the *denticulation* of the wall blocks, meaning the way they fit together. Artificial stones, such as brick or lime sandstone, are laid in a *masonry bond pattern*, one of a number of arrangements for placing the individual brick or stone courses (layers). Natural stones, depending on their composition, size, and shape, are placed for optimal denticulation and bonding. With rectangular base material, we need to follow masonry bonding principles. The mason needs to create a puzzlelike structure with a well-fitted joint design when working with bulky

Right: Field wall with distinct inverted shape; boulders and slab-shaped broken material was used. Cumbria, Northern England.

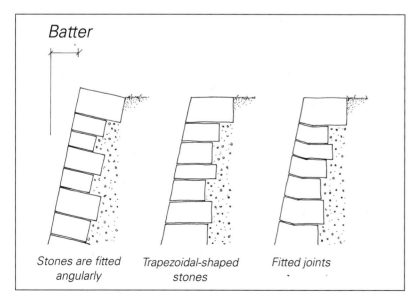

Batter

Stones are fitted angularly

Trapezoidal-shaped stones

Fitted joints

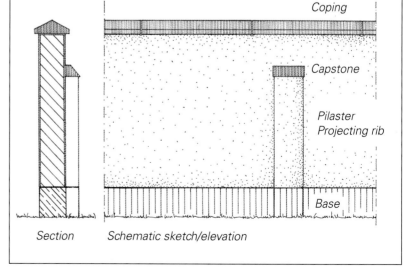

Coping

Capstone

Pilaster
Projecting rib

Base

Section

Schematic sketch/elevation

rough stones and round material like boulders and river stones. Careful walling up creates a visible outer area that is even, without protruding bosses or hollows. Here the erection of batter boards or working with a profile gauge is very helpful.

While clinker brick walls, concrete walls, and plastered walls are always built vertically and with a rectangular cross section, stone masonry, when used for supporting walls, is executed with either *a wide base gradually transitioning to a narrower coping* or *battered, with a ratio of rise to run depending on the material used and the total height of the wall.* Battered walls are inclined toward the slope by 10 to 15 percent to better absorb shear force. With a wall that has an inverted shape, the gradual forward tilting that occurs over decades because of earth pressure is hardly noticeable. On the other hand, a wall that was built to be exactly vertical but is visibly tilting forward because of earth pressure not only looks unattractive but is unstable and in danger of collapsing.

Coping

For structural and planning reasons every wall needs a solid top, a *coping*. This upper wall closure can be an accent element or a rather inconspicuous secondary detail. In most climates, walls must have a cover to keep rainwater from penetrating and to prevent frost damage. The execution of the coping

Saddle-shaped plain tile

Mono-pitch plain tile

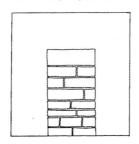
Coping without overhang

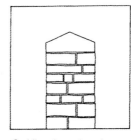
Saddle- shaped coping

Half-round coping

Coping with overhang and drip nose

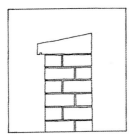
Mono-pitch coping

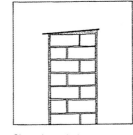
Sloped steel plate

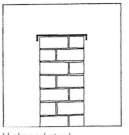
U-shaped steel

Metal flashing

has to be well thought out. It influences the wall's appearance considerably and, in the long run, determines its stability and intactness.

Copings for stone masonry

There are many possible designs for stone masonry copings. The simplest and most traditional is the *capstone.* An upper wall closure with a thick final layer of great anchoring depth and rather long stones demands exceptional technical skill. Custom fitting guarantees that the joints are sealed for the entire depth. The various course depths of the capstones are integrated seamlessly into the masonry bond. The character of the masonry bond, up to the top, is consistently retained. A coping done this way has no overhang.

For walls with batter the coping is given the same inclination as the wall. To drain off the water, the capstone is placed at an angle. Supporting walls drain toward the slope. The capstone can also be a saddleback-shaped roof over semiround ashlars. Capstones on dry-placed walls contribute substantially to the overall stability of the structure because of their own dead weight and their denticulation with the masonry bond.

A rowlock capstone on a dry-placed wall, found worldwide in the field walls of many farming communities, adds a special character. For the rowlock, similar stones are piled as a consecutive course across the full width of the closure. While the masonry shows a horizontal coursing structure, the rowlock course is vertical or angled. The coping is stabilized by

Top left: Shed-roof-shaped cover with a titanium zinc metal plate 0.2 inches (0.5 cm) thick.

Top right: Rowlock of saddle-shaped clinker bricks.

Second row left: Gutter-shaped upper edge of a concrete wall.

Second row right: Steel sheet cover

Third row left: Rowlock of semicircular cast brick.

Third row right: Natural stone coping with underlay of crest tiles at joints.

Fourth row left: Rowlock coping on a cantilevered layer of plain tiles.

Fourth row right: Inverted U coping of 9-gauge (0.15 inches or 4 mm thick) galvanized sheeting.

wedging or angular positioning. Often the stones of the rowlock overhang a few inches on either face of the wall, so that a deep overlay is guaranteed. Originally these types of wall were created to enclose grazing land. The often abrasive and spiky rowlock has the advantage of preventing grazing animals from climbing over the fence.

The rowlock coping can have very different structures depending on the materials used. If untreated fieldstone boulders are used, the capstones appear accordingly rough. If fine schist sheets are used, a beautiful, graceful wall closure can be created. The appearance is always shaped more by the stones used than by the workmanship. Today copestones are the most common treatment on stone masonry walls. The copestones are from the same natural stone material as the wall itself. They

are purchased as prefabricated elements, in lengths of 3 feet (1 m) or more, with the surface treated with bush hammers, dressing tools, or roughening tools.

It is essential to ensure that the size of the coping matches the stratification, height, and joint design of the stone masonry wall. With walls more than 3 feet (1 m) high, the cover sheets should be 3 to 4 inches (8–10 cm) thick. A cover that is too thin feels unsatisfactory, while one that is too thick visually crushes the wall. When the wall is covered for its entire width with stone, it is very well protected from penetrating water. Only the seams at the joints constitute weak links; therefore they need to be joined with special care.

Most covers are done with overhang. They should always have a *water drip* or *weather molding* on the underside of the longitudinal groove that is worked

into the sheet, so that water drains away before it reaches the surface of the wall. For walls with batter, a level covering is recommended, and the overhang needs to be extremely large to keep the dripping water away from the wall effectively.

Unfinished masonry coping
Unfinished (uncoated or unsealed) masonry walls—for example, those made from brick or lime sandstone—are traditionally finished with a *rowlock,* a course of upright stones. The rowlock must be absolutely free of cavities and cemented carefully. Under no circumstances should perforated clinker bricks be used. Unfinished brick or limestone with rowlock is standard in England, the Netherlands, Denmark, and northern Germany. It is not frostproof because of its many joints, so it can only be recommended with reservations for most regions of Central Europe, but pre-cast concrete or limestone copings of various shapes, stone coping, and brick or rowlock are popular in the United States. In any case, a crown with coping, such as steel plate, protects much better against penetrating water than rowlock.

Left: The rolling contour of a stone masonry wall blends in ideally with the surrounding landscape. Tucson, Arizona.

Right: The upper six sketches show different profiles of the top edges of walls. The lower six sketches show different possibilities for the line layout of the ground plan.

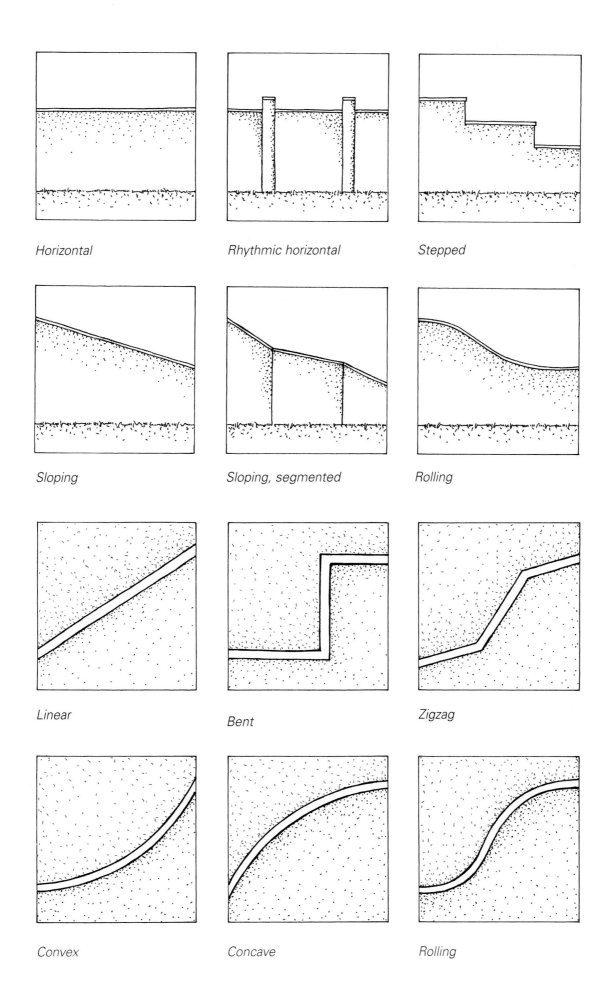

Horizontal

Rhythmic horizontal

Stepped

Sloping

Sloping, segmented

Rolling

Linear

Bent

Zigzag

Convex

Concave

Rolling

Coping for plastered walls

An impermeable cover is especially crucial for plastered walls. The water that enters between plaster and stonework inevitably creates enormous damage and ugly chipping. A cover of stainless steel, zinc, or aluminum sheet is a solid solution for the problem and will look fine with the right planning and execution. We do not recommend copper because it often leaves greenish stripes and stains on the wall surface. Steel plate covers must be well proportioned. They must include expansion joints at intervals of about 16 feet (5 m), and the sections must be perfect, without any dents, or the overall result will be unsatisfactory. As a rule, wood fastened to the wall is covered with sheet metal. It is advisable to use U-shaped sections so that the cover doesn't have to be screwed on; the necessary drilling creates weak links where water can penetrate.

Prefabricated covers of stone masonry or concrete slabs are technically acceptable, reasonable, and very common. The slabs must be sloping, and they require an overhang and drip molding. The splices between the single elements are the weak spots. Mortar joints break open quickly under the impact of frost, allowing water to penetrate through the cracks. This problem cannot be solved satisfactorily with permanently flexible pointing material; synthetic pointing materials such as epoxy do not last long outdoors and tend to become heavily soiled due to high UV impact. Mortar joints are preferable, but the splices should have an underlayment of a V-shaped metal plate or a barely visible semicircular plastic channel to divert water from above to the outside. The joints should not be too small, but an ample 0.3 inches (0.76 cm) so they can be jointed flawlessly with mortar. It is of the utmost importance to create a small drip molding in the mortar joints with the trowel. Lead fillings are a very beautiful but very expensive way of jointing. Today, lead joints are used only with very high quality landmarked structures.

Copings with brick covers—special-purpose bricks as well as plain clay roofing tiles—were very common in the 1950s and 1960s. This type of coping is rustic-looking and is only advisable if it matches its environment stylistically. From a structural design standpoint, it is a very reliable, permanent, and fairly inexpensive solution.

Expansion joints

Many walls are long, and here we need to keep in mind the temperature-related aging process of contraction and expansion. We need to plan *expansion joints* at regular intervals of 16 to 26 feet (5–8 m). These function as predetermined breaking points and prevent cracks from forming in the masonry.

Planning basics

When designing a wall, the designer thinks of functionality, construction, and optimal appearance. A wall can blend in with its environment and continue the stylistic characteristics of that environment, either historic or modern. But a wall of a certain size can also be a self-contained element and create a purposeful counterpoint to its surroundings.

Walls as design elements offer many possibilities. They require planning considerations beyond the selection of materials. In addition to the proper dimensions, a pleasing linear layout is an important element of design.

Height

When designing a wall we ask ourselves what the right and proper height is. Rather than using measurement units—feet or meters—to describe height in the planning stage, it is better to think of categories such as knee-high, table-high, shoulder-high, and above head-high. These correspond to heights of about 18 inches, 2 feet, 5 feet, and above 6 feet (40, 70, 150, and above 180 cm). These ways of presenting height choices are often clearer to clients than abstract numbers, and help prevent them from being unhappy with the height after the project is finished. For all parties involved, it may be helpful to model the wall on location with a combinations of lath strips, lengths of rope or cords, cardboard, or panels on a scale of 1:1. This way, the design can be evaluated before construction starts.

To find the right height the overall context must be considered. A shoulder-high wall might feel too strong and unpleasant some places; in other places it might not create sufficient separation.

With retaining walls that are used for topographical design, the overall height can be partitioned into several lower walls, called stepping. This is often much more attractive

A rough stone wall 9 feet (2.75 m) high is beautifully structured with clearly defined horizontal courses and vertical expansion joints. Dublin, Ireland.

than exaggerating the difference with a single excessively high well that does not fit the scale of the site.

Thickness
The required thickness of a wall depends on the load it has to carry. If you are uncertain, discuss the thickness with a structural or civil engineer. For freestanding walls in particular it is important to find harmonious proportions. Depending on the material that is used, the wall might look too massive or too thin. In considering the wall's thickness we need to think of the cover or coping as well, so that the two can be coordinated. With freestanding walls, the endpoints and passageways especially, the adjustment of wall height, thickness, and cover is visible in the profile, so it has be resolved in an aesthetically pleasing way.

Walls on a slope
As elements of garden and landscape architecture, walls must often respond to topography. A wall along a slope frequently has a stepped horizontal contour that needs to be planned carefully on the basis of terrain sections.

New walls in gardens and landscapes are definitely perceived as structures. Therefore they have to follow the laws of geometry; they demand, depending on the material, a certain perfection, right-angularity, and vertical and horizontal layout. The horizontal joints of the stonework are aligned with a level horizontal plane, even if the wall's overall contour deviates from the horizontal. Only in specific landscape environments, and only with stone masonry walls or in particular, clearly intended artistic settings, does the eye accept wall contours that depart from the horizontal. In contrast, it is understood that field walls follow the groundlines and are not restricted to horizontal contours.

Legal concerns
Another factor that must be taken into account in designing a wall is adhering to the zoning code or planning laws.

In Germany these issues are ruled by the *Landesbauordnung* (state building code). The height of a wall bordering adjacent property is determined by the *Nachbarrechtsgesetz* (Neighboring Rights Act), which is different in each state. In most states enclosing walls—called "*dead*" *enclosures* as opposed to hedges—are allowed up to a height of 4.9 feet (1.5 m). A higher wall must be moved back from the boundary, with the setback distance equal to the measurement by which the height has exceeded 1.5 meters. In the United States, walls are regulated by the local building code and zoning laws: the maximum wall height, the minimum setback from the property line, and even the materials permitted for construction may all vary from place to place.

Builders often fail to consider that the foundation cannot protrude past the property line. To avoid this overstepping, the foundation may be planned with an angular profile, the so-called L-shaped foundation discussed earlier.

Knee-high

Table-high

Shoulder-high

Above head-high

The gardens and walls below the seventeenth century
Stockalper Palace have been completely restored. Brig, in
the canton of Wallis, Switzerland,

Field walls built with boulders and rough
slabs in Cumbria, Northern England

Stone masonry walls

Stone masonry walls

Stone masonry walls are favorites in garden and landscape construction because of their attractive natural surfaces, their durability, and their beautiful character, which improves with age. The appearance of a stone masonry wall is influenced not only by the materials used but also by the quality of the workmanship. Until the Industrial Revolution, because of the difficulty of transporting materials, stone masonry walls were most often built from stones that could be found locally. In many regions, field stones collected from the bordering fields were used in wall construction. Today, natural stone is a commodity traded worldwide, and stones for walls are transported over huge distances.

The DIN 1053 standard (in the U.S., ASTM WK52) determines the requirements for stone masonry. It distinguishes among dry-placed walls, rubble stone walls, cyclopean masonry, hammer-dressed, irregular, and regular coursed masonry, ashlar masonry, and facing masonry (called *masonry-supported stone cladding* in the CSI standards). The boundaries between the individual categories of walls cannot be defined exactly, however. With stone masonry walls more than with any other type, the craftsman's experience is more important than the standards.

We differentiate between freestanding, *double-* and *single-sided* stone masonry walls; the latter are retaining walls with only one exposed surface and backfill on the other side. The professional terminology includes words like *runner* and *runner stone* (also *stretcher*), and *bonder* or *bonder stone* (also *tie stone*). A runner doesn't extend through the entire depth of the wall; it has only one exposed surface and is joined by other stones on the back side. Bonders span the entire wall and, in the case of a double-sided wall, are exposed on both sides. *Bonding* refers to the backfilling of butt joints in single stone courses and, accordingly, the covering of the butt joints with an additional stone course. According to standards, at least 4 inches (10 cm) of bonding is needed with stone masonry walls. Therefore, butt joints can never be directly on top of one another; they must always to be staggered. Cross joints are not allowed. Another word common in the professional terminology is *inverted cavetto* (or *batter*), the continuously narrowing or wedge-shaped wall profile typical for natural stone. The supporting wall is clearly tilted toward the slope, as it gains more stability this way.

Stone masonry retaining walls are frequently backfilled with concrete. We then speak of a *backfilled concrete wall*. Contrary to *walls with facing* or *cladding*,

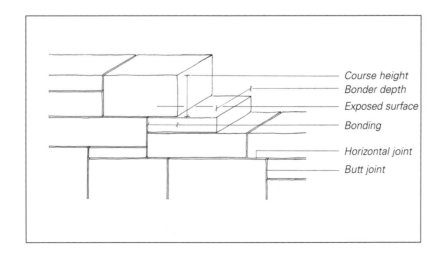

— Course height
— Bonder depth
— Exposed surface

— Bonding

— Horizontal joint
— Butt joint

Left: The technical vocabulary for stone wall construction includes terms like: course depth, bonder depth, exposed surface, bonding, horizontal joint, and butt joint

Right: The walls of the Northwest Cemetery in Karlsruhe, Germany, are granite, with a saddle-shaped coping. Their rolling contours fit perfectly into the landscape.

concrete and stone masonry interlock during backfilling and thus form a structural unity. A modern system of forms (molds into which the concrete is poured) is not necessary to backfill stone masonry walls. On the front, the stone masonry serves as the form; on the slope side, a form can be created with square timber and simple panels.

Like dry-placed walls, stone masonry walls should get a solid cover to prevent penetrating rainwater, frost damage, and efflorescence. The execution of the coping has to be well planned because it will protect the appearance and intactness of the wall for years to come. The use of *coping stone slabs* is very common. An overhang with drip molding and incline is technically the best solution. A beautiful traditional cover is the *cover stone*. It fits seamlessly in size and finish into the overall appearance of the wall. The treatment of dry-placed walls with heavy cover stones or rowlock serves primarily to guarantee the stability of the overall construction.

Dry-placed walls

Dry-placed walls, seen in many European cultural landscapes, are rooted in regional traditions. In areas that are lacking timber, such as Ireland, England, Wales, and Scotland, but also in Apulia, the Balearic Islands, and the Cyclades, grazing fields are often enclosed by dry-placed walls because material to build wooden fences was unavailable. In many European areas where grapes, olives, and fruit are grown, sloped areas are terraced with dry-placed walls in a manner typical of the region. In the Alps, too, primarily in Switzerland, Austria, and Italy, we find excellently executed dry-placed walls. The craftsmen's traditions were revived by the construction of railroad tracks in the nineteenth century; the standards and rules corresponded remarkably well with theoretical foundations of engineering.

The DIN 1053 (ASTM C 119) standard sets forth the requirements of professional masonry. It demands the bonding of butt joints, and that two *stretchers* (laid lengthwise) be followed at least by one *header* (laid

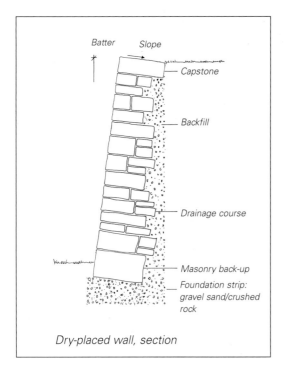

Dry-placed wall, section

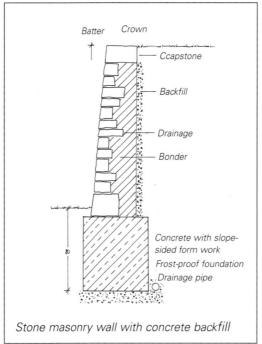

Stone masonry wall with concrete backfill

Top right: Dry stone cemetery wall with saddle-shaped top-stones as wall coping. Bolton, Cumbria, northern England.

Bottom right: Field walls of rough stone slabs. Cumbria, Northern England.

crosswise). The DIN standards specify: "The rough stones have to be fitted in the correct masonry bond with little processing and without the use of mortar, so that there will be narrow joints and small cavities. The cavities between the stones must be filled by smaller stones in such a way that wedging creates tension between the wall stones."

This means that with dry-placed masonry the bond, positively tied, is created solely by friction and interlocking. The craftsmanship shows in the appearance of tight, consistent joints. Extra-wide joints are always wedged with small *rock spalls*. They are put in place as part of the construction, not added later for cosmetic reasons.

Freestanding dry walls are traditionally 3 to 5 feet (1–1.6 m) high. Depending on the material, at the foot they are 20 to 31 inches (50–80 cm) wide. The ideal proportions of a wall cross-section (wall height to wall width) are between 1:0.33 and 1:0.5. Dry-placed walls are built with a batter of 10 to 15 percent. A wall 5 feet (1.5 m) high and 30 inches (75 cm) wide at its foot has a coping width of 12 to 18 inches (30–45 cm).

For dry-placed walls that are used as supporting walls, generally a height of 5 feet (1.5 m) is the maximum, although we find examples of much higher walls in the technical literature of engineering. The batter of retaining walls is usually much more distinct than that of freestanding walls; it is about 15 to 20 percent. The wall's center of gravity is shifted in favor of higher stability; less material and a narrower coping in the direction of the slope is needed

Dry-placed walls should be backfilled with material that drains well, intercepts storm water runoff, and withstands hydrostatic pressure. The resulting impact of force—especially during frost—is kept away from the wall. As a rule, the base material for the construction of dry-placed walls may be slightly modified in advance or used as is. The builder works each stone on location and as needed to achieve high stability and an exact fit. The broken pieces can serve for rock spall in the backfill.

Depending on the base material, a variety of wall surfaces are possible: anything from fine slate courses to unshapely blocks in combination with small filler stones can be used. Most satisfying, despite today's transport possibilities, are walls made from materials typical of the region, because these fit beautifully into the environment.

The copings of dry-placed walls are usually done with large-sized cover stones. Their high dead load is crucial for the wall's stability. Often a rowlock course is used. The structure and joint design of the continuous rowlock stand out clearly from the joint design of the wall itself. This creates a charming overall appearance.

Because they are relatively flexible structures, dry-placed walls resist settlement, so an elaborate foundation is not needed. Small changes in the masonry bond caused by settling are not apparent to the eye and do not result in structural damage. Dry-placed walls gain beauty and patina as they age. They do have to be maintained regularly; small repairs will be necessary here and there in order to prevent deterioration.

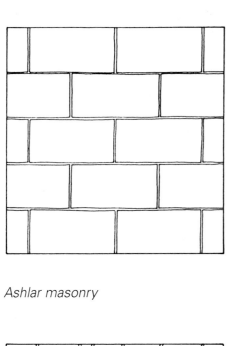

Ashlar masonry

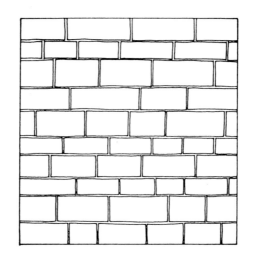

Coursed ashlar masonry

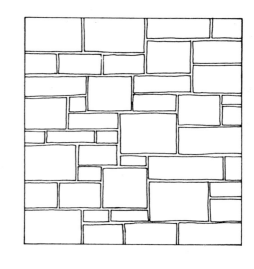

Random ashlar masonry

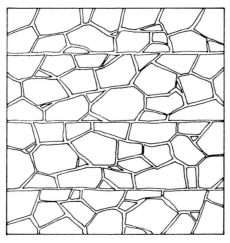

Random rubble in courses

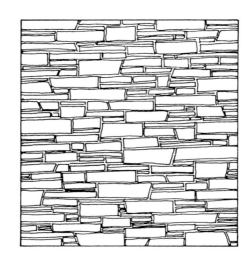

Slate rubble masonry

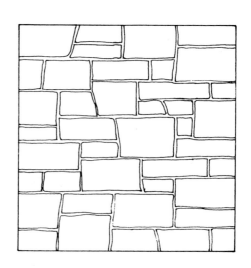

Hewn coursed masonry

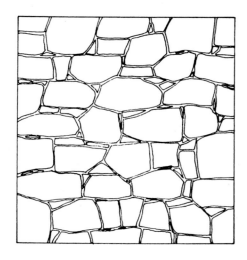

Rock spall rubble masonry

Mixed masonry

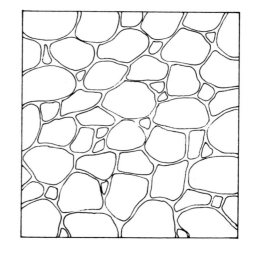

Random rubble masonry

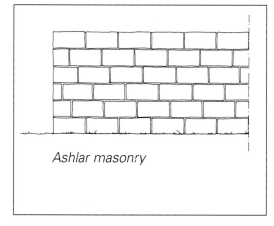

Ashlar masonry

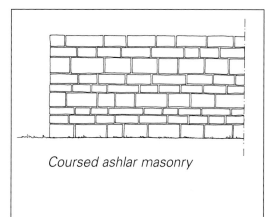

Coursed ashlar masonry

Random rubble masonry

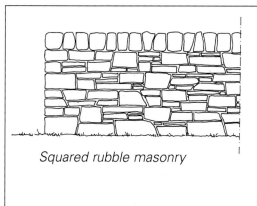

Squared rubble masonry

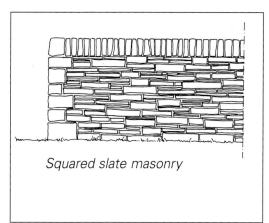

Squared slate masonry

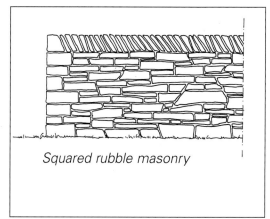

Squared rubble masonry

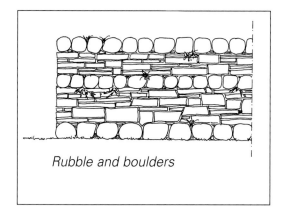

Rubble and boulders

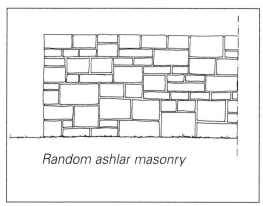

Random ashlar masonry

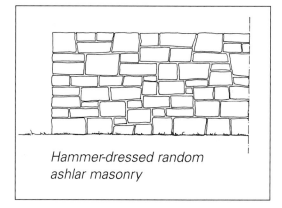

Hammer-dressed random ashlar masonry

Above: Cyclopean wall of Raumünzach granite at the Heidenstück cemetery colony, Karlsruhe, Germany.

Top left: Low enclosing wall of a country house in Maine

Center left: Oyster-shell limestone wall with angular surface area, made from ashlar-type rubble. The base material was presorted by height and fitted in horizontal layers. Backnang, Germany.

Bottom left: Natural cleft oyster-shell limestone wall in irregular arrangement. The skilled reworking of the material insures an exactly fitted and harmonious joint design. Itzlings, Germany.

Dry-placed walls of split blocks

For some time, the stone masonry trade has offered large natural stone blocks for rustic dry-placed walls. Depending on the supplier, these stones, for which no standards exist, are called *split blocks, ashlar blocks,* or *wall blocks.* The material, usually granite, shell limestone, or Jurassic limestone (in some regions also brownstone or yellow sandstone) is not—like many other natural stones—transported over long distances, but is usually brought from nearby stone quarries. For the use of these natural stone blocks, we generally follow on the rules for dry-placed masonry, the DIN 1053 (ASTM WK52) standards.

Walls built with large natural stones are correspondingly large. They have a rough appearance and are therefore not advisable for every project. Large-sized natural stone material can be used in landscape architecture to secure slopes and to construct retaining walls that run parallel to the street. But in garden architecture it can only be recommended with reservations. Walls from split blocks turn easily into fortresslike bulwarks. They take up a lot of space and can visually overwhelm a residential garden.

The blocks are split on all sides except the visible face, which has a natural cleft surface. At times, traces of the rock drill can be seen. A coarse material that breaks into bulky layers is especially well suited for the extraction of split blocks. The length of the stones varies among suppliers; most are between 20 and 60 inches (50–150 cm)

wide and between 12 and 24 inches (30–60 cm) high.

We aim for uniform height, so that we can erect technically solid dry masonry. But the lengths of the stones should vary considerably. In order to achieve a lively, not too regular overall appearance. The longer the stones in relation to the course height, the more successful and attractive the courses. The exposed faces of the single stones should always have a distinct elongated rectangular format—the length of the stone should be at least 1.5 to 2 times the height of the stones. If the exposed faces are too square, the overall appearance will not be aesthetically appealing. Moreover, the stability of the wall is not guaranteed because the courses are not staggered. The staggering of butt joints needs to be at least a third of the stone's length.

Walls of split blocks are usually fitted without mortar. Therefore they are dynamic structures based not on a concrete foundation set below the frost line, but on an *unstable foundation*—a strip of gravel and gravel sand 12 to 16 inch (30–40 cm) deep. The top edge of the strip foundation should be covered by at least 4 inches (10 cm) of soil. The foundation should be 4 to 6 inches (10–15 cm) wider than the wall.

Because of the high dead weight, dry walls of split blocks are especially well suited to waterside and embankment fortification. A square yard (1 m^2) of masonry weighs (depending on material and anchoring depth) between 1 and 1.5 metric tons, and this high dead weight offers the advantage of great stability

with professional setting. The blocks on a construction site can be moved only with the appropriate machinery; it is an arduous process, and builders are unwilling to make small repairs later on. The construction machinery cannot be used everywhere; in some situations its use is inadvisable, because it can cause unwanted soil compaction that will have a negative impact on future vegetation.

When we carefully choose and sort and the stones in advance—still best done in the quarry before delivery—an almost exact fit with relatively small joints is achieved. If necessary, stones can be worked in the quarry to render the material usable for solid coursing. This step is often left out because of time constraints or the lack of professional skill. When a client has not specified the standards for the material, this additional effort seems unnecessary. Once the blocks are delivered contractors will do their best. They might even fill large joints with mortar or soil, which leads to instability or even collapse of the wall in the long run.

Walls of split blocks must always built with a distinct *batter*; that is, the layers of the masonry will slant from the courses beneath by 2 to 4 inches (5–10 cm). This leads to a slightly stepped cross section. For reasons of stability the stones are fitted with a slight batter toward the slope.

If the ground makes this necessary, dry-placed walls from split blocks can be built with a longitudinal incline of about up to 10 percent. If the incline is greater, we need to install steps accordingly.

Above: Large split blocks of limestone as a waterside wall. Neumarkt, Oberpfalz, Germany.

Right: Large split blocks of granite in the Wall Park, Berlin.

Dry-placed walls of boulders and river stones

In some regions of central Europe dry-placed walls of boulders and cobble stones are common. Often the stones were the only masonry material available. The boulders in the moraine areas shaped by the Ice Age in northern Europe and at the edge of the Alps made a long journey among the detritus of the glaciers and were polished to a round shape like cobbles.

Because this material is often of different geographic and geological origin, we might find very different natural stones next to each other.

The dry, mortarless laying of glacial boulders and cobble stones requires great technical skill. The stones seldom need to be hewn, but coursing them skillfully demands a lot of patience and a keen visual sense.

Boulder and pebble walls are usually constructed as retaining walls. Because the stones have rounded surfaces, there is hardly any friction, so the walls are always especially wide, and not very high, with a batter of 20 to 30 percent. Walls of rounded boulders are common on the Frisian Islands and in the landscapes near the shore of Lower Saxony and Schleswig-Holstein in Germany, so we often call them Frisian walls.

Dry-placed walls of glacial boulders are traditional in the gardens and landscape architecture of Scandinavia. This residential garden sketch is by the Swedish garden architect Gunnar Martinsson.

Top right: Dry-placed wall of boulders excavated on location during construction work. Garden of Schloss Klessen, near Friesack, Mark Brandenberg, Germany.

Bottom right: Wall of boulders, Hillerød cemetery, Denmark. Burials take place directly in front of the wall. The names and birth and death dates engraved on the boulders are the only indications of the graves.

Rubble stone masonry walls

Rubble stone masonry is the term used for walls made from rough or broken stones. These walls are bonded and the interstices filled with mortar. There are double-sided freestanding rubble stone walls and single-sided retaining walls of rubble stone.

The thickness of the masonry wall depends on the height of the wall and the static demands. It should be at least 20 inches (50 cm). The rubble stones are processed more or less to fit the harmonious masonry bond. The appearance of rubble stone walls is strongly influenced by the material used and the resulting joint appearance. The joints can have a maximum thickness of about 1 inch (3 cm). Coursed rubble material is mostly used, so the majority of the horizontal joints are level and the majority of the butt joints are vertical. For a lively overall appearance, it doesn't matter that once in a while single butt and horizontal joints run at a slant. As a rule, rubble stone walls are built with a horizontal top that doesn't follow the ground level but is stepped.

When we use non-horizontal natural stones such as lava chunks, boulders, or large river stones, we get a polygonal, irregular joint appearance. The resulting wall is called a *cyclopean rusticated wall*. In the history of architecture there are many examples of extremely well done, permanent cyclopean walls—for example, in the buildings of the Incas in Peru or those of the Etruscans in Italy. Cyclopean walls are built to this day on Mallorca and other Mediterranean islands, where the available natural stones do not allow any other method. Cyclopean walls do not need a horizontal top edge; they can follow the ground level without problem, and regular steps are not necessary.

In contrast to dry walls, set on a *frost barrier* made from compacted gravel or rubble sand mix, mortared rubble stone walls that are fixed constructions have to be based on a frost-resistant concrete foundation with expansion joints at regular intervals.

A wall erected at the base of a hill must have a built-in drainage pipe set below the upper edge of the foundation, with adequate slope for drainage. If hydrostatic pressure is expected, selective diagonal drainage needs to be considered. This is often omitted, and inadequate relief of hydrostatic pressure endangers the wall.

Coursed masonry

In contrast to rubble stone masonry, natural stones for *coursed masonry* are worked more extensively and hewn into a relatively regular, rectangular format. The types of coursed masonry are *hammer-dressed, irregular*, and *regular.*

In hammer-dressed coursed masonry, single stones are reworked to achieve almost horizontal joints and vertical butt joints. The height of the stones changes within one course. The single courses have differing heights, generally decreasing from bottom to top. Walls of hammer-dressed coursed masonry can also have slimmer cross-sections than rubble stone walls. According to standards, the minimum thickness is about 20 inches (50 cm); the maximum joint width is about 1 inch (3 cm).

For irregular coursed masonry, stones are worked at the horizontally- and vertically-running joints and butt joints at a minimum depth of 6 inches (15 cm). The joint width at the exposed surface is a maximum of 1 inch (3 cm). The height of the stones changes at times within a single course, so that we see offsets in the joint design.

With regular coursed masonry the heights of courses vary, but each course has a consistent continuous height. The joint width at the exposed surfaces is a maximum of 1 inch (3 cm). We make the utmost use of the stones' strength in regular coursed masonry; therefore, the wall can have a very slim cross-section. For freestanding stone masonry walls in regular coursed masonry a thickness of 9 inches (24 cm) is sufficient according to standards; 12 inches (30 cm) is recommended.

Ashlar masonry is a regular coursed masonry with masonry wall blocks of almost equal measurements. This type of wall, which hardly satisfies our aesthetic expectation of stone masonry, was quite common in ancient times. For example, it can be found in Hadrian's Wall in England. Today ashlar pattern masonry is occasionally manufactured from industrially processed natural stones.

Outstanding, beautiful stone masonry walls can be found
everywhere in Provence. Nowhere are they as attractive
as in the small towns of Gordes in the Vaucluse region of
France. Characteristic here is the cream-yellow limestone
from quarries in Lubéron and a coping with a rowlock of
upright stone slabs.

Mixed masonry

As a rule, stone masonry is built continuously from the same stone material. However, there are some examples of mixed masonry, a type of wall that offers a charming contrast: the combination of natural stones and bricks, or dark and light natural stones, often arranged in alternating stripes. Coursed rubble stone and boulders can create very interesting effects. In some English landscapes there is a tradition of dry stone walls into which slabs of different stones have been fitted in regular intervals as continuous binders, resulting in small decorative stripes (below left). The artist and architect Charles Jencks has played with this motif in his private garden (center) at Portrack House in Dumfriesshire, Scotland. He worked delicate, ascending bands of red sandstone into a newly erected dry-placed wall of gray sandstone.

The same effect can be created with stone masonry walls with brick courses or marble strips at regular intervals. Occasionally we can find these details in historic Italian town walls.

The combination of stone masonry and concrete is another possibility. As soon as a wall has developed some patina, the change in the material is hardly noticeable, as is illustrated by the Stuttgart IGA wall shown on page 71.

Especially with high walls, the horizontal separation achieved by alternating materials creates a beautiful effect. Wall with ocher and blue-gray sandstone in the garden of Barrington Court, Somerset, England.

Wall with boulders and red sandstone slabs at Portrack House, Dumfriesshire, Scotland.

Garden wall of basalt, brick and glazed recycled materials, Rowallene Gardens, Northern Ireland.

Right: The concrete band is not only a structural necessity; it also beautifully divides the limestone wall and visually reduces its height. Eichstätt, Bavaria, Germany.

Walls in the Edwardian style

In art history, it is common to identify different style epochs with names of the rulers at the time; hence, in England, the Elizabethan (sixteenth century), the Jacobean (seventeenth century), the Georgian (about 1762–1830), the Victorian (about 1842–1900), and, last but not least, the Edwardian, named for King Edward VII (1901–1910), which actually lasted until the end of World War I. The prewar Edwardian era was a time of great economic prosperity, wealth, and brisk construction activity. Many country homes were built with gardens, and although the architects and landscape designers often resorted to historical models, they merged them resourcefully in new and unique expressions. Walls and hedges had been important in garden design for a long time. Whether artful parterres, rose or shrub gardens, vegetable gardens, or fruit orchards, the Edwardians leaned toward *walled gardens* designed as garden spaces surrounded by walls or shrubs. Walls and shrubs give the garden its frame; they carry the architectural order, and offer protection from the wind. Enclosing walls were a very important element, especially in the Edwardian era.

The Edwardian architect Thomas Mawson valued garden walls because they could be planted. His book *The Art and Craft of Garden Making*, first published in 1900, devotes an entire chapter to planting walls. Mawson recommends forty different species of plants suitable for this use,

including twenty-four different clematis and thirty-six types of rambler rose.

Also noteworthy are the walls planted by Gertrude Jekyll (1843–1932) and Edwin Lutyens (1869–1944). "A Lutyens house with a Jekyll garden" was the epitome of refined taste in the Edwardian era. Lutyens designed the buildings, the spatial order of the garden, and the structural details. Jekyll detailed the planting and controlled the overall appearance. An experienced artist and a profound connoisseur of history and garden art, she had a highly evolved sense of style and an overall perspective. In 1889, the forty-five-year-old Jekyll met the twenty-year-old Edwin Lutyens. They worked together for decades on more than a hundred large garden projects. Some of these gardens are considered among the most important garden artworks of the twentieth century.

Many of the country houses designed by Edwin Lutyens are well preserved, but only a few of the gardens created by the team of Jekyll and Lutyens can be found today in their original state. The foremost is at Hestercombe House near Taunton in Somerset. Created around 1906, it is one of the most important examples of the team's work. The garden was restored extraordinarily well a few years ago, and some areas have been replanted according to the original planting plan. Well-preserved garden walls of Edwin Lutyens are at the gardens of the country houses of Greywalls, near Edinburgh, Folly Farm, near Reading, and Abbotswood, near Stow-on-the-Wold.

Lutyens's great love of details is evident in the walls he designed. He paid a lot of attention to structural details—the coping, the corners, the design of height differences. When appropriate, he integrated wall niches, medallion-shaped cut stones, and windowlike openings.

In his walls Lutyens played creatively and innovatively with mixed materials and different colored natural stones. He created charming structures by fitting in classical decorative elements and unusual materials—for example, plain clay roofing tiles, thin slate sheets, or shiny chunks of firestone. From today's perspective, we can say that some design ideas found in the walls of the artist Andy Goldsworthy (see pages 60–61), or in walls made from recycled materials (see pages 130–31), were anticipated by Lutyens.

Gertrude Jekyll propagated *wall gardening*, the adding of perennial bushes to stone masonry walls. Later, Karl Foerster (1874–1970), German plantsman and perennial grower and breeder, also recommended this. The walls in the gardens of Lutyens and Jekyll were often lushly planted with yellow corydalis (*Corydalis lutea*), Spanish daisy (*Erigeron karvinskianus*), catmint (*Nepeta* x *faassenii*) or red valerian (*Centranthus ruber*).

Top: Wall niche with bench, an example of the highest craftsmanship. Hestercombe Gardens, Somerset, England.

Bottom: Refined radial fitting of slate rowlock. Greywalls, East Lothian, Scotland.

The Stuttgart School

The Killesberg area near the western edge of the Stuttgart valley, in Germany, originally a quarry, was redesigned as a public park in 1939 for the German Garden Show; 54,000 square feet (5,000 m²) of walls and stairs were built, including about 5,000 steps, and almost 200,000 square feet (18,000 m²) of paving were laid. The high-quality craftsmanship of the stone masonry is culturally and historically connected to the surrounding vineyards. These works at Killesberg, in the style of what came to be called the Stuttgart School, became a tremendously influential model that influenced gardens, especially in southern Germany, until the 1960s.

Garden shows in 1950, 1961, 1977, and 1993 changed parts of the Killesberg Park, but some of the characteristic retaining walls and flights of steps from the 1939 redesign, in red sandstone, remain unchanged today.

Adolf Haag (1903–1966), the central figure of the Stuttgart School, was a leading force in the Killesberg work. In the 1950s and 1960s, he was one of the most renowned garden designers in southern Germany. No one was more skilled in executing stone masonry work. He developed his design ideas mostly on location, working without blueprints and always supervising the work personally. Since he aimed for a design close to nature, he constructed tall garden walls as dry-placed walls. He had the wall stones split from large stone chunks on the construction site, gave them a clean, rectangular exposed surface, and then laid the walls. With the sandstone that he frequently used, the placing and adjusting of the newly broken, still wet stones was rather easy. Like traditional vineyard walls, the dry-placed walls of the Stuttgart School followed certain rules: a foundation depth of 8 to 16 inches (20–40 cm) when they are built on undisturbed subsoil. The foundation is built on a gravel frost barrier with large-size foundation stones. The desired relation of wall thickness to height is 1:3; the minimum thickness is 12 to 16 inches (30–40 cm). The backfilling has to be done carefully and with large stones. This was easily realized on the Killesberg project because plenty of suitable material was available in the former quarry. To guarantee the stability of the dry-placed wall, a third of the stones are binders, stones that span the entire wall depth.

With dry-placed walls, as with natural stone coping, the harmonious overall appearance results from the joint design— that is, the execution of the masonry bond. The first design rule for dry-wall construction in the style of the Stuttgart School is that the thicknesses of the stone courses tend to decrease from bottom to top. The second rule is that the wall stones must have a distinct shape with proportions of 1:2 to 1:5. Vertically placed stones cannot be used because they would destroy the harmonious appearance. The occasional installation of *changers* or *changer stones* is desirable because it enlivens the overall appearance. A changer is a stone with an approximately square face. Two stone courses are set on one or on both sides of the changer.

The upper wall closure is done with heavy cover sheets or capstones that stabilize the wall with their high dead weight. The dry-placed or dry stone walls of the Stuttgart

No cross joints in the masonry bond

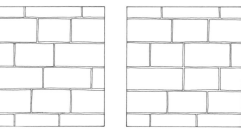

Right   Wrong

Avoid long butt joints

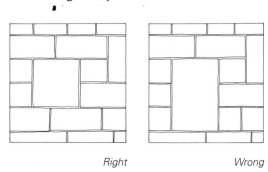

Right   Wrong

Right: The walls and stairs of red sandstone in Stuttgart's Killesberg Park are of extraordinary artistic quality.

Below: The bonding of steps and stringer are masterfully done. The capstones of the stringer are hewn perfectly.

School were built, for structural and design reasons, with a 20 percent batter.

The town of Stuttgart trains many young landscape gardeners in the Killesberg area. Therefore the important tradition of dry-placed or dry stone wall construction continues to be taught. Repairs, maintenance work, and the occasional erection of new, smaller sites are done to this day in the style of the Stuttgart School.

The stone masonry walls of Ian Hamilton Finlay and Andy Goldsworthy

Some artists elevate to works of art craftsmen's traditions that have been maintained throughout the centuries. The work of Adolf Haag, with its roots in south German vineyard walls, can be considered such works of art, and so can the works of the Scottish artists Ian Hamilton Finlay (1925–2006) and Andy Goldsworthy (born in Britain in 1956). The dry stone field walls we find in many British cultural landscapes become poetic art in their hands. Finlay is best known for his own large garden, built between 1966 and 2006, in the solitary landscape of Scottish Larnarkshire, about 37 miles (60 km) south of Edinburgh. This complex of four acres that Finlay named Little Sparta is a small, natural, pastoral magic kingdom with countless philosophical and literary references. It entices visitors to go on an exploratory walk and to try to decipher the many stone tablets, with their word games, twists, and ironies. Sir Roy Strong, the renowned critic of British

garden art, calls Little Sparta "the only truly completely independent garden creation in Great Britain since 1945."

In several places in Finlay's garden, stone masonry in the traditional style is elevated to art by tablets integrated into the wall. On one wall a tablet quotes a Gaelic poet: "Se toiseach is deireadh an duin a' bhuachailleachd"; on the other side of the wall we find the English translation: "The beginning and the ending of life is herding." Thinking about these words, we might perceive these field walls that enclose grazing land in a different way: not as stone structures, but as gestures of guarding and watching over.

In another part of the garden Finlay built a traditional sheepfold with natural stones. The sign reading "Eclogue" on the entrance's

wooden gate is a reference to the eclogues of the Roman poet Virgil, translated into English in the nineteenth century by Samuel Palmer in a book illustrated with pastoral English landscapes. Stepping into the sheepfold we find three tablets and read "Folding the last sheep." Sheep and shepherd are Christian symbols, so we might interpret the text as the shepherd caring for the last sheep. Reflecting on

Right: Ian Hamilton Finlay's "Eclogue" installation in the garden of Little Sparta inspires us to reflect on ancient literature, but also refers to a landscape dominated for centuries by sheep.

Below: In Ian Hamilton Finlay's garden, field stone walls, typical of the region, are elevated to works of art by the insertion of tablets. Pictured is his "Little Fields–Long Horizons." Little Sparta garden, Ayrshire, Scotland.

the tablets in Finlay's garden engenders connections to literature and makes us think of the surrounding landscapes, which are often sheep meadows, in a different way.

Goldsworthy sculpts all over the world—in Scotland, England, France, Japan, and the United States—with natural materials like sand, earth, stone, ice, moss, fern, wood, or blossoms. Sometimes his creations last only a few hours or days, but they are documented in photographs, videos, and books.

Many of Goldsworthy's works can be considered land art. They are a very creative and playful grappling with nature and landscape, nearly always closely connected to their location, whether that is sparsely inhabited Cumbria in northern England or the adjoining Dumfriesshire in Scotland. There are no signs pointing out these creations as works of art. They stand outdoors as silent objects and are sought out by connoisseurs willing to make the pilgrimage.

In Goldsworthy's work artistic stone masonry is very important. The artist designs the wall and craftsmen with whom he has been working for years execute the design. Goldsworthy describes his stance: "I want a simple (but beautiful) wall. . . . It is for me to put the walls where they will take on new meanings that articulate the changing relationship between people and place. These meanings are made stronger because the walls are agricultural. Although my walls are not entirely bound by the demands of agriculture it was important that my first was made as a practical response to the need to divide a piece of land. I must keep the walls' roots firmly in agriculture, not art; otherwise, they lose their meaning as works of art. I enjoy the aesthetic of the practical. . . . The enclosures that are part of my first wall have their origin in those used by hill farmers to gather sheep. I enjoy the feeling upon entering them—sometimes for shelter on the open and windswept fell. The space is made quiet and intense by the containing wall, giving a sense of protection and care" (Andy Goldsworthy, *Stone* [New York: Harry N. Abrams, 1990]). Modern man too experiences this primal emotion when he enters one of the squares enclosed by Andy Goldsworthy's walls.

Below: The walls of a restored sheepfold of artistically designed natural stone composition, a project of Andy Goldsworthy in Eden Valley, Cumbria, England.

Right: Andy Goldsworthy's installation "Storm King Wall," 1992, meanders for more than half a mile through a forest. Storm King Art Center, New York.

The first segment of the Parque de Cabecera, 44 acres (18 ha) in area, opened in 2004 in the northwestern end of the green belt of Valencia, Spain. In the former riverbed of the Turia, it runs for 6 miles (10 km) through the town. The river had repeatedly caused devastating flooding in the past and was rerouted at the end of the 1960s as a canal. Wide areas of grass and water, rows of trees, and beautifully executed stone masonry of light limestone are the main characteristics of this park. With their well-designed, interesting contours and the overall concept the walls here achieve the status of art.

Walls of stone masonry palisades

Round timbers strung together to form walls, fences, or barriers are called palisades. They are familiar to us from ancient and medieval fortress construction. In the 1970s palisades were "discovered" as design elements in garden and landscape architecture. In private gardens and public complexes, round timbers, usually pressure-treated, were often used to stabilize small differences in height.

As fast as this fashion took hold, it disappeared. The lifespan of timber is limited despite waterproofing. Often single round timbers rotted in a few years, and replacing them was costly or physically impossible.

In the middle of the 1980s, the building material industry developed concrete palisades, which are still manufactured and for the most part have replaced wooden ones. They come in round or square cross sections. They are superior to the wooden palisades because they last longer, and their preformed shape results in an optimal bond between the individual elements. Concrete palisades are often a functional and inexpensive solution, but landscape architects and demanding clients do not favor them because they are considered a cheap, mass-produced solution.

In the 1990s granite palisades, mostly imported from Asian quarries, became available. These soon found many fans because of their crafted natural appearance. In dimensions and proportion, they resemble the quarry-produced *curb stones* and *molding stones* long employed in road construction but not suitable for use as palisades. Because these had only two processed surfaces, satisfactory butt joints could be executed.

Most clients, especially private clients with elaborate house gardens, prefer the granite palisades over concrete palisades despite the higher price. Natural stone is considered of higher quality, and there is no doubt about this given its long lifespan. Granite palisades are used for small supporting walls, for terracing, to back up hedges or enclose flowerbeds, and as pointed steps in stair construction. If high enough, they protect from wind and provide a visual barrier.

Granite palisades are a standardized product in the construction materials trade. Depending on the supplier, rectangular palisades are offered with cross sections of 3 x 8 inches (8 x 20 cm), 4.75 x 9 inches (12 x 22 cm) or 4 x 10 inches (10 x 25 cm). The square palisades usually have a cross section of 4.75 x 4.75 inches (12 x 12 cm). The individual lengths are between 12 to 98 inches (30–250 cm). The surfaces of the palisades are either split or finely bush-hammered. Not as common are palisades from other natural stone materials. They can be special-ordered, but are much more expensive than the mass-produced ones from the Far East.

Palisades must have a frost-resistant foundation, at least with walls of more than 31 inches (80 cm) in height. The single elements are set in a foundation of earth-moist lean concrete (C 12/15; 1750 psi) approximately 8 inches (20 cm) high, then adjusted with a mallet, straightedge, and level, and temporarily fixed with scaffolding, planks, roof battens, and bar clamps. Following this, they are stabilized on each side with a concrete shoulder. The anchoring depth should be at least a third the length of the overall palisades. That means we can produce a palisade 4 feet (1.25 m) long with a 31-inch (80-cm) high supporting wall.

The joints between the palisades are never completely closed; with heavy rain unwanted washing out may take place. Therefore before backfilling the palisades, a bituminized board, foil or, best of all, a dimpled plastic sheet should be inserted. The backfill material must be water-permeable, meaning gravel, crushed rock, or a coarse recycled mix. To offset hydrostatic pressure, we need to build a drain pipe and connect it properly. Only the upper area, after an interlayer of polypropylene landscape cloth is installed, is filled with soil and plant substrates, so that the plants located directly behind the palisade have space for their roots.

As an alternative to the common wall with upright adjacent granite palisades, supporting walls of up to 24 inches (60 cm) can be coursed horizontally and bonded. To get very small joints, bonding mortar should be used. The material needed is twice as much with horizontally fitted palisades, but because of the wide coping—10 inches (25 cm) instead of 3 to 5 inches (8–12 cm)—it may look much more attractive and might fit our notion of a "correct" wall better than the slim upper edge of a palisade.

Above: Horizontally fitted granite palisades in a front garden. Grötzingen, near Karlsruhe, Germany.

Right: Vertically fitted granite palisades in a house garden in Karlsruhe-Durlach, Germany. The change in grade, totaling 6 feet (1.8 m) in all, is absorbed by three parallel walls. The lowermost wall consists of L-shaped stones, which are hidden by a hedge.

Walls of crust slabs

Crust slabs are a byproduct of the process of producing different natural stone materials in the quarry. After blasting, large blocks are cut or sawed open for further processing. The first cut separates the so-called crust, with its natural cleft surface. It is often still marked by chisel traces. Depending on the type of stone, this crust is more or less textured and of varying thickness. Normally the stonecutters try to keep the crust segments as thin as possible because they are considered a waste product. But thicker slabs can be cut to order. They then fulfill the constructional and static demands of use as wall panels.

Crust slabs are primarily used to support rather small height differences. The natural cleft surface is the exposed surface, and the sawed back side fits in against the soil. The crust slabs are anchored like natural stone palisades in a concrete foundation. In contrast to palisades, crust slabs can achieve large overall length. If the construction site is easily accessible they make economical supports.

If crust slabs are to be used for free-standing walls, the question of what to do with the smooth back side arises. For enclosures, the slabs can be fitted alternately, so that there is no proper front and back side; both exposed sides of the wall will have the same appearance.

With adequate height and surface texture, crust slabs always appear rustic. In the countryside, when the walls are not too high, they create wonderful surfaces that contrast with the architecture and the green of vegetation. They satisfy a demand for high quality, and their potential uses of are almost inexhaustible.

Wedge-shaped leveled grass areas are enclosed by thick crust slabs. Nnear Potsdamer Platz, Germany.

Angularly fitted crust slabs of shell limestone make an ideal protection for trees. Sindelfingen, Germany.

Right: A rough-looking but very creatively designed wall from rough crust slabs spans the precinct of the Lycée du Pic Saint-Loup in Saint-Clément-de-Rivière, Hérault, southern Franceschool. The natural stone immediately seems to belong to the landscape. Most of it came from the excavation and landscaping on the site. Pic-Saint-Loup in Saint-Clément-de Rivière, Hérault, outhern France

Below: Rustic enclosures with rough sandstone crust slabs. The slabs, placed alternately front and back, reveal a natural cleft and rough-sawn surface. Rüthi, Rhine Valley, Switzerland.

Walls with stone masonry cladding

Walls with stone cladding consist of a reinforced wall, typically of concrete with all its structural advantages, and a cladding of stone masonry that gives it aesthetic qualities.

As we have seen, with stone masonry the technical and structural limits are soon reached; if a wall is to be more than 5 feet (1.5 m) high, has high earth pressure, a high load, or hydrostatic pressure, natural stone walls are not advisable. We expect functionality and durability for decades from an expensive, newly erected wall. Therefore the construction needs to be very solid. In many of the situations listed above this is only possible with the help of reinforced concrete.

If an exposed concrete surface is not desired, a wall with stone masonry facing is a suitable solution. The concrete wall fulfills the structural demands and the stone masonry cladding the desire for an attractive visible surface.

Walls with a veneer are generally used when huge earth pressure has to be absorbed. The concrete retaining wall behind the cladding has to be engineered; the dimension of the armoring iron and the foundation measurements are determined accordingly. The side facing the ground must be protected against hydrostatic pressure. Drainage mats, which are readily available, are useful only if they are fastened solidly at the upper edge of the wall with a top rail. In addition, the drainage mats must be backfilled with material suitable for draining. This filter package must be protected with filter fabric, or it will gradually disintegrate into fine particles and lose its ability to drain. At the top edge of the foundation a drainage pipe is placed, with sufficient pitch to carry the runoff to lower ground or into a storm drain.

A common method is the cladding of concrete walls with natural stone slabs 1 to 2 inches (3–5 cm) thick. Usually the plates are glued or fastened with anchors that are drilled in horizontally. But it is always obvious that the natural stone is merely cladding, because it hangs in front, almost like wallpaper.

A correct cladding, on the other hand, depending on the wall height, is 3 to 12 inches (8–30 cm) thick and is not glued on. Ideally the cladding is an independent and self-supporting second layer. It thus gives the impression of a real stone masonry wall, the impression of massiveness. The cladding is either directly connected to the load-bearing wall or built as a ventilated front wall with about a 1 inch (2–3 cm) gap to the concrete wall. It is anchored to the load-bearing wall with stainless steel anchors; according to DIN 1053, five anchors per square meter are required. In the United States, the 2008 Masonry Standards Joint Committees (MSJC) code distinguishes between different types of anchors. The spacing varies accordingly, but typically it calls for an area not greater than 2.67 square feet (0.25 m^2) per tie. A great advantage of ventilated cladding is that transmission of efflorescence from the concrete wall to the stone masonry is almost impossible.

To emphasize the impression of massiveness it is advisable to cap the wall with substantially sized natural stone slabs that are at least 2 to 3 inches (6–8 cm) thick and to glue corner pieces at the wall edges wherever they are visible. The glued seam, its quality and durability guaranteed by the supplier, is hardly visible, and so the appearance of a massive natural stone wall is created.

Cemetery walls in Chur and Munich-Riem
Exceptional walls with stone masonry cladding have been erected around the urn burial plots of the new Fürstenwald cemetery in Chur, Switzerland. The artistic design does not downplay the construction material—concrete—but rather makes it part of the surface design: precast concrete parts in the form of stylized branches separate the exposed areas from the rubble masonry cladding. A thin steel plate cover caps the wall and blends in well with the lively colors of the rubble stone.

The extension of a cemetery on the sparse grounds of the Munich-Riem Park was completed in 2000 by landscape architects Ursula Hochrein and Axel Lohrer. Wide, neglected grasslands and a wall enclosing burial islands characterize this park. Heavy doors made from Cor-Ten steel, used to cover many burial fields, and dry-placed walls of Austrian and Bulgarian gneiss are the design elements of this modern cemetery complex. Because of the coursed stone structure,

Above left: The combination of stone masonry and artistically designed precast concrete parts in the form of stylized branches creates a charming overall appearance.

Above right: The walls near the buildings of Munich-Riem's new cemetery are clad with slabs of broken gneiss. In combination with the L-shaped concrete walls, they achieve a unique precision.

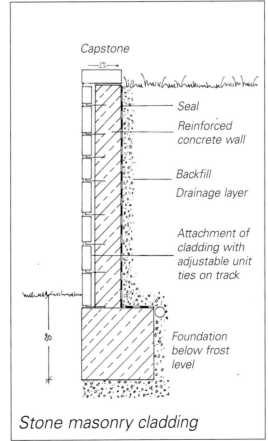

Capstone

Seal

Reinforced concrete wall

Backfill

Drainage layer

Attachment of cladding with adjustable unit ties on track

Foundation below frost level

Stone masonry cladding

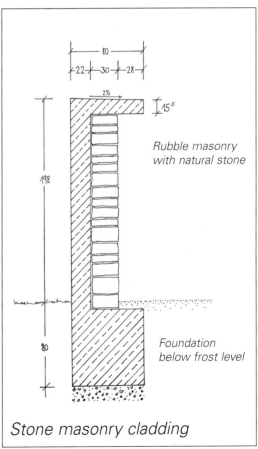

Rubble masonry with natural stone

Foundation below frost level

Stone masonry cladding

the surfaces of the dry-placed walls look like coursed masonry. Their intense coloring changes from gray to rust to black-brown. Andreas Meck and Stephan Köppel, the architects of the chapel and side building, worked with the theme of stone masonry as the facing for concrete walls. In keeping with their stark, minimalist architecture, they wanted to avoid a rustic appearance. The wall cover is cleverly designed, using an upside-down L-shaped concrete wall.

The Stuttgart IGA walls
For the new design of Killesberg in Stuttgart for the International Garden Show in 1993, the landscape architects Luz and Partner developed a new wall system, the IGA wall. A prefabricated concrete skeleton is mounted against the terrain with 10 to 15 percent batter, or slope, and bolted together. Its horizontal beams will be visible, while the vertical columns will be hidden because of their setback.

The strong horizontal concrete band, which is 6 inches (15 cm) thick for structural reasons, creates beautiful separations, especially with higher walls. For the foundation a smooth strip of lean concrete on a frost barrier is sufficient.

The interstices of the module, which is 3 feet (1 m) high and 6 feet (2 m) wide, are filled with stone masonry in dry construction. The precast concrete parts guarantee the wall's static strength, while

The Stuttgart IGA wall; the stacked precast concrete parts alternate with stacked courses of stone masonry. Stuttgart, Germany.

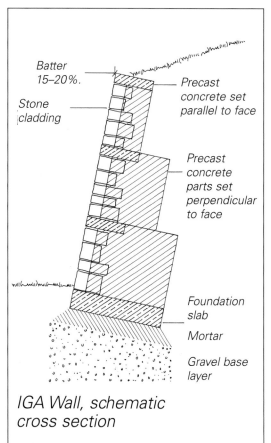

Batter 15–20%.

Stone cladding

Precast concrete set parallel to face

Precast concrete parts set perpendicular to face

Foundation slab

Mortar

Gravel base layer

IGA Wall, schematic cross section

The IGA walls erected in Stuttgart in 1993 for the
International Garden Show are made from prefabricated
concrete frame parts filled in with several courses of stone
masonry. They demonstrate that even industrially made
concrete parts can be combined very well with natural
stone.

the filling offers the ecological and visual advantages of dry stone masonry walls. Although the IGA wall has not been as widely utilized as its manufacturers had hoped, those in Stuttgart are of high quality in design and craftsmanship and have held up very well. They remain in fine condition, and seem more pleasing and more traditional than walls made from gabions filed with natural stone (see pages 114–18).

Kunsthalle Würth in Schwäbisch Hall
Kunsthalle Würth, an art museum in the small southern German town of Schwäbisch Hall, opened in 2001 after a two-and-a-half-year construction period. It was designed by the Danish architect Henning Larsen, who won the international competition for the commission. Kunsthalle Würth houses the collection of the German industrialist Reinhold Würth as well as other changing exhibitions.

The new building is located in the medieval old town in the area of a former brewery. The design was strongly influenced by the pronounced hillside location and the surrounding historical buildings. The four-story building fits perfectly into the medieval town and, at the same time, is outstandingly modern. Especially distinctive are the fine horizontal lines of the stone masonry façades as well as a prominent umbrella in front, a construction made of steel and glass.

The traditional shell limestone known as Crailsheimer limestone, with a noble yellow tint, was used for the numerous supporting and enclosing walls as well as for the design of the façades. The shell limestone is mined in numerous nearby quarries. It is a good frost-hardy, weather-resistant material. Its color and its dense, homogeneous structure create an attractive overall image. With the horizontal stratification of the natural stones, the designers referred to the geological stratification in a quarry.

The walls of the structure as well as the walls in the landscape are made of reinforced concrete and outfitted with stone masonry cladding. This cladding is 5 inches (13 cm) deep at the top edge of the single limestone blocks and is secured with stainless steel anchors to the concrete core. With an even course height of 7 inches (17 cm), the single cut stones are between 12 and 35 inches (30–90 cm) long. To achieve the distinctive lively play of the wall surfaces, the limestone was prepared in the quarry with a method especially developed for this project. A block of stone, sawn on all sides, is split with the help of a wedge-cutting machine perpendicular to the sediment layers. The structural characteristics of the shell limestone create a convex fracture, because the pressure of the wedge finds the path of least resistance. The convex part

of the broken cut stone is what is used; the concave remainder is reserved for other uses. It is impossible to predict in what direction the fracture will curve. Therefore, the piece to be sawed is centered under the wedge to get at least one usable part.

After the convex surface is produced, the cut stone is sawn in half; the lower half is turned around so that, when they are stacked, the two pieces form overhanging layers (see the illustration). The top edge of the natural cleft surface, the part where the spitting wedge was placed, is nearly straight. If needed, this line may be reworked. The bottom edge has an irregular, rolling structure; the overhang achieves interesting height and shadow effects. Here, no further reworking is necessary after the industrial manufacturing process.

The coursed surface structure at channels and corners is especially interesting toward the entrance court because the natural cleft surface borders on sawn areas. The intricate vertical stratification can be seen from the side and is thereby accentuated.

Kunsthalle Würth received honorable mention in the German Stone Masonry Competition of 2001. The jury especially praised the modern use of traditional materials as well as the accenting of the natural stone character with the help of an industrial production process.

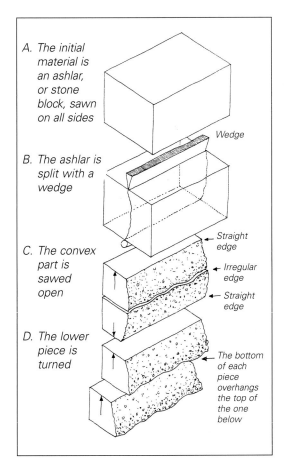

A. The initial material is an ashlar, or stone block, sawn on all sides

Wedge

B. The ashlar is split with a wedge

Straight edge

C. The convex part is sawed open

Irregular edge

Straight edge

D. The lower piece is turned

The bottom of each piece overhangs the top of the one below

Diagram of the creation of cut limestone used at the walls of Kunsthalle Würth, Schwäbisch Hall.

Right: The scale-like stepped split ashlars of limestone described opposite were used for both façades and outdoor walls at Kunsthalle Würth.

Blocks of Franconian limestone were sandblasted to create a set of steps with 3-inch (8-cm) risers. The foundation was done with poured-in-place concrete and forms, together with the core of the stringer—a precast concrete part—a structural unity for the absorption of earth pressure.

Top right: Sandstone facing of a wall in the government district on the bank of Spree River. Berlin, Germany.

Bottom right: A difference in height of about 27 inches (70 cm) in the garden of a residence in Neumarkt, Oberpfalz, Germany, was absorbed with a concrete wall 8 inches (20 cm) thick, with a facing of Franconian limestone 4 inches (10 cm) thick.

The undulating top edge makes this wall into a playful element. BUGA (Bundesgartenschau or National Garden Show) 2005, Munich, Germany.

Concrete walls

Concrete walls

Concrete walls are today's most cost-effective and easy solution for walls in open spaces. Concrete is often judged hastily as aesthetically inferior, banal, and ordinary, but with good design and execution we can build distinctive, beautiful walls with this material too.

In many situations concrete walls are an appropriate design element. They offer a satisfactory contemporary appearance so long as the material has been processed professionally, expansion joints have been carefully constructed, and all edges have a chamfer. But concrete walls are only reasonable in cost when prefabricated parts or standardized framework or forms can be used. Also, the construction site has to be accessible to transportation for the delivery of ready-mix concrete. To be cost-effective, the overall construction project has to have a minimum scale. If elaborate formwork has to be built and if the concrete has to be transported by wheelbarrow to the site it's best to compare the price with other construction methods.

But it is not just the price that influences the decision to build with concrete. Often concrete can be easily combined with other available structure materials. Many shapes and surface structures can only be achieved with this multifaceted building material.

Basically, we distinguish between walls made from industrially produced precast concrete elements and walls from poured-in-place concrete. In both cases, surfaces can be flat or can be constructed by a specific type of formwork. For the most part, when it is poured in place the concrete is of quality C 20/25 (former classification B 25) (3190psi). For precast parts concrete is generally of quality C 30/35 (former classification B 35) (4350psi); it makes the surfaces of the precast parts appear flatter and finer. The surface of poured-in-place concrete can also be made perfectly flat if we use formwork and high-quality concrete, and the areas are later sanded and waterproofed.

Surface design
The choice of material used for the formwork—rough boards, for example, or other materials with textured surfaces—determines which interesting effects will permanently define the surface of the concrete wall. Often linear textures or striations are created that accentuate the wall horizontally or vertically. We can apply two-dimensional materials to the formwork that will be cast in reverse on the concrete surface. In designing the concrete walls of the Chur cemetery, for example, the garden architect Dieter Kienast used pine needles in the formwork to create lively textures.

Concrete may be colored with added pigments or certain aggregates to achieve a pronounced change from the standard gray.

In addition, walls can be bush-hammered, by using a square-headed hammer with spikes, to create a rough, lively surface. The mineral aggregates, mostly shiny pebbles, are exposed and as a result make an interesting outer texture. After the finish, the appearance can be changed by applying special colored glazes or coatings.

Sometimes it is necessary to treat the concrete wall after construction because the exposed concrete does not turn out to be of the desired quality. In this case sandblasting

Flat–concrete wall with rolling top edge. BUGA (National Garden Show) 2005, Munich, Germany.

Washboardlike surface texture of a concrete wall. Vaduz, Liechtenstein.

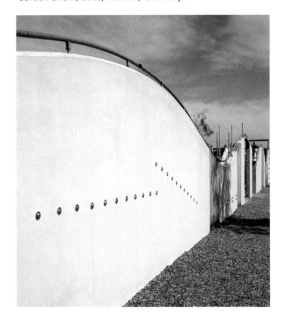

Right: Glass bricks integrated into a concrete wall in a regular grid pattern give the wall transparency despite its height and solidity. Forum 2004, Barcelona, Spain.

Below: The concrete walls of the Scottish Parliament have a decorative, filigreed surface that resonates with the textures of bent ash-wood panels in front of the building's glass façades. Edinburgh, Scotland, 2004.

Below: Bolts and butt joints of many standardized concrete formwork elements leave pronounced marks in the concrete, thereby creating decorative surface patterns. Parc André Citroën, Paris.

Top left: Flat concrete wall with integrated viewing slot, Bremer Landesvertretung (Representative Office for the State of Bremer), Berlin.

Center left: A flat concrete wall is partially painted, so if just that portion of the wall is likely to become dirty, for example because of soiling from exhaust fumes, a separate cleaning or repainting can be done.

Bottom left: The strong stone masonry coping is the characteristic element of this distinctively structured concrete wall. BUGA (National Garden Show) 2005, Munich.

or glazing is to be considered in lieu of hiding the unsatisfactory surface under coating.

Walls near parking spaces are often soiled by exhaust fumes. To be able to clean the dirty area occasionally or to cover it with a protective coating, the lower part of the wall can be articulated by a strong base created by inlaying a batten into the casing (see page 80, center). This way, the entire wall surface does not have to be treated.

Unfortunately, concrete develops a *patina* as it ages. Unlike the traces of age in natural stone, the patina here is bothersome and looks shabby. The aging process can be slowed down considerably by covering the top with a hot-dip galvanized steel sheet that is fitted at a slant. Usually concrete walls are constructed without an overhang and drip lip. Even a simple slant at the top of the masonry wall coping to divert the water toward the ground is rarely done. Thus the dirt and dust particles that settle on the top cover after each rain run over the wall surface and leave visible traces. On a flat wall they are much more noticeable than on a textured concrete wall or a stone masonry wall. In a garden or a park this visual defect can be masked well by growing climbers such as ivy (*Hedera helix*) or Virginia creeper (*Parthenocissus quinquefolia*).

Long drab concrete walls benefit from screwed-on trellises or latticework that adds texture to the wall and enhances its appearance. In choosing climbers we need to pay attention to whether they will hold onto the wall surface or whether they should only be planted on a trellis. The traces of the anchoring roots of ivy or the countless adhesive disks of the climbing Virginia creeper remain on a wall even after the plants are uprooted or pruned back. The joy produced by fast-growing, lush, green plants may turn to deep disappointment with the dirty or damaged wall surface. However, some species of vines, like *Clematis*, are less problematic, particularly if they are trained on latticework or trellises.

Three-dimensional design
Concrete is better suited for three-dimensional design than any other material. Concrete walls can be covered in any contour as long as the claddings and reinforcements used allow this. Rolling shapes on a blueprint are just as possible as spirited contours on a wall's top edge.

Three-dimensional shapes can also be achieved with objects inlaid in the formwork. In the outdoor spaces at the Scottish Parliament in Edinburgh, designed by Enric Miralles and Benedetta Tagliabue of Barcelona, are lively concrete walls that have been created by inlaying pipes. Today artistically designed, relieflike concrete surfaces are rare, but simple, graphic inlaid patterns are a common and easy design method. High concrete walls are often outfitted with horizontal inlaid slats that give them an attractive texture.

Openings in the wall—"windows" or "spy holes"—offer bold effects with little effort if glass blocks are fitted into the form. An overpowering protective wall becomes a light, transparent design element that nevertheless fulfills the demand for cohesiveness.

Structural advantages
Unlike dry-placed walls, concrete walls are entirely rigid fixed constructions. They must be based on a deep concrete foundation set below the frost line, and they must be fitted at regular intervals with expansion joints. No other wall can absorb earth pressure as well as walls made from reinforced concrete. The concrete wall is securely bonded to the foundation with *starter bars*, so it will not tilt vertically. The dimensions and alignment of the steel or rebar are determined by structural calculations.

Concrete walls are thinner than other walls. Freestanding concrete walls up to 6 feet (1.8 m) high can be done in poured-in-place concrete with a thickness of about 7 inches (18 cm), or in prefabricated parts with a thickness of about 6 inches (15 cm). For concrete walls of 6 feet (1.8 m) high with earth pressure, a thickness of about 12 inches (30 cm) is needed. If the plans call for walls with larger dimensions, the time for discussion is during the early design stages.

The crown
Even though a concrete wall is not a masonry structure, it is a monolithic mass. Therefore we can do without a cover in designing and constructing it. A plate cover is usually added only if we want to protect a glazed or painted wall surface from dirt, as was described earlier. A cover keeps the dust and dirt that settles on the wall from leaving ugly stains.

The cap of a retaining concrete wall can be constructed with a slight incline toward the slope so that the water drains off to the back. The wall top can be formed as a gutter, so that the collected rainwater drains at the wall heads and other selected points.

Right: In the so-called Spurengarten (garden of traces), an intimately designed area planted with perennials, the ochre-colored concrete looks like stone masonry. Spreebogenpark, Berlin.

Below: Wall of colored concrete showing the impress of rough-sawn plank formwork. The wall is covered by a screwed-on steel plate, 0.3 inches (8 mm) thick, set in neoprene. Neumarkt, Oberpfalz, Germany.

L-shaped precast concrete walls

Today, erecting supporting walls with L-shaped units, is a common and useful construction method. Manufacturers offer the precast parts, made of reinforced concrete, in depths of 18 inches (45 cm) to 10 feet (3 m) and widths (overall lengths) of 20 inches (50 cm) or 3 feet (91 cm). The L-shaped cross section and the load of backfill on the foot stabilize the precast parts in a simple and practical manner and secure them against tilting. The foundation and bracing require much less effort than comparable walls of poured-in-place concrete.

The higher the L-shaped unit, the wider the foot (that is, the short leg of the L); a unit that is 18 inches (45 cm) high has a foot about 1 foot (30 cm) wide; a 10 foot (3 m) high unit has a width of 6 feet (1.8 m). For structural reasons the units are reinforced above a certain height; the wall then has a slightly wedge-shaped cross-section. The thickness at the top of the unit (depending on the manufacturer) is between 4 and 5 inches (10–12 cm); the reinforced type increases thickness to 6 to 8 inches (15–20 cm).

Most manufacturers offer special parts, such as inside or outside corner elements with different elbows, or convex or concave quarter arches.

L-shaped units are also available with a variety of exposed surfaces. The flat exposed concrete surface is standard, but there are also units with plank structure or a finish that simulates stone masonry facing—the concrete surface is coated with colored natural stone chips and then sandblasted.

Manufacturers offer the product with testing for typical dimensions, so structural calculation is not needed. For walls above 8 feet (2.5 m), a backup structural calculation must be done that takes into account local conditions such as the type of backfill material and subsoil, the impact of load from traffic areas above the wall, and the entire batter system.

The foundation for L-shaped units is either a *simple foundation* or a *frost-free foundation*. For construction depths of up to 31 inches (80 cm), a foundation 1 foot (30 cm) deep is sufficient unless hydrostatic pressure is a factor, or extremely cohesive or sandy ground demands special attention. The foundation trench is filled and compacted with a sub-base of 4 to 6 inches (10–15 cm) of frost-resistant material (such as lean concrete with uniform aggregate size or concrete with a highly compacted aggregate mix). The units are then set up in a 4-inch (10-cm) thick underlay made from earth-moist lean concrete (C12/15) (1740psi).

L-shaped units of more than 31 inches (80 cm) construction depth must have a frost-deep foundation. A coat of earth-moist lean concrete, 8 to 12 inches (20–30 cm) thick, stripped horizontally, is applied to a layer of compacted aggregate material 20 inches (50 cm) thick. After the lean concrete hardens, the units are staggered with a coat of cement mortar 1 inch (3 cm) thick. With a construction depth of up to 6 feet (2 m), the units can be moved on the construction site with a front-end loader, and then adjusted with a mallet and level. The individual precast parts are set and then connected to each other. On the back side are steel eyes used for transport and to hold the round steel bars with which the components are bonded together. Before backfilling, the back side of the butt joints is covered with bituminized board or plastic dimpled sheet, so that no fine particles can be flushed out. If plants are planned in back of the units, good water drainage is necessary. To avoid waterlogging, and for water retention, it has proven useful to install a layer of chipped bricks or expanded clay with a thickness of about 8 inches (20 cm) at the base of the units. Frost-sensitive plants should not be planted directly behind these units since their roots are exposed to frost directly behind the concrete; frost can also penetrate from above and from the side.

L-shaped units are a contemporary and essential element in garden and landscape architecture today. They are a popular, cost-effective construction material that is readily available and easy to fit. The parts are easily transported with the machinery common in garden and landscape construction.

If desired the concrete can be easily concealed with planting. In this case, the L-shaped units function solely as a retaining wall; the planting determines the garden design. Especially for formal compounds, evergreen hedges, such as yew and box, are recommended. A planting of trailing and overhanging plants such as ivy is possible if only a small area for planting is available.

For very high formal demands, the head of the L-shaped units can be concealed. A specially manufactured Z-shaped steel part (see drawing, opposite, plugged onto the unit, makes it possible to bring the adjoining area closer to the barely noticeable steel edge. The unwanted concrete top edge of the precast part disappears. To do this the L-shaped unit needs to be installed deeper than the height of the mounted facing, a requirement that must be taken into account in the planning stage.

Tegel Castle, Berlin. The conversion of a farm building into an apartment building made a 6-foot (2-m) deep trench necessary. The grade change is absorbed by a brick wall and a wall of concrete L- shaped units (visible in the top picture). The L-shaped units are concealed by an evergreen yew hedge; the lower photo was taken on the day of the planting.

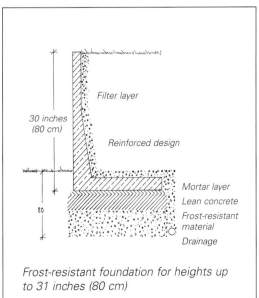

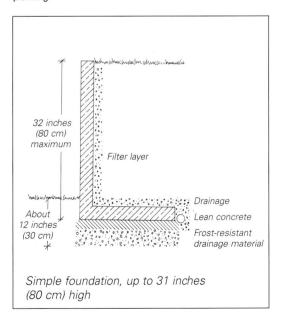

32 inches
(80 cm)
maximum

Filter layer

About
12 inches
(30 cm)

Drainage
Lean concrete
Frost-resistant
drainage material

Simple foundation, up to 31 inches (80 cm) high

30 inches
(80 cm)

Filter layer

Reinforced design

80

Mortar layer
Lean concrete
Frost-resistant
material
Drainage

Frost-resistant foundation for heights up to 31 inches (80 cm)

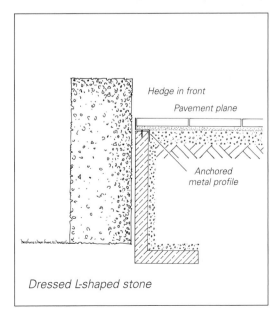

Hedge in front

Pavement plane

Anchored
metal profile

Dressed L-shaped stone

A brick wall encloses a school's vegetable garden.
Parc de Bercy, Paris

Clinker brick walls

Clinker brick walls

Clinker-brick walls have distinct regional traditions. *Clinker* is a term describing a hard-fired brick used for walls and pavements. Its dimensions and manufacturing process are unique in terms of temperature of firing and the coatings that may be applied. In the United States bricks have different dimensions than the metric-based units in Europe. A standard brick in American practice is commonly 7⅝ x 3⅝ x 2⅝ inches, although there are many variations. Paving brick and brick that is used in exterior walls is fired at a higher temperature than bricks for interior walls and other uses not subject to weather and strong compressive forces. Brick walls are common in areas where no natural stone material was available for wall construction, for example in northern Germany, Denmark, and the Netherlands. Brick construction was common in the Roman Empire. Today we still find bricks, despite often amply available natural stones, everywhere there were Roman settlements, including many regions of Italy and Spain.

Common bricks are fired at 1652° F (900° C), clinkers at 2372°F (1300° C). The higher temperature creates sintering, a glazelike melting of the surface, and the brick achieves high density and pressure resistance. Clinkers absorb hardly any water and are therefore mostly frost-proof, unlike regular wall bricks, which always need a protective finish or some other type of coating outdoors. As a rule, they are elutriated—that is, with a thin coating applied as finish—as *fair-faced masonry.* Elutriating is a traditional surface finish that is very important in historic preservation. In elutriated fair-faced masonry, the joint grid recedes into the background and becomes an unobtrusive structure.

All of the important rules and regulations covering clinkers and bricks—the compression strength classes, bulk density, and frost resistance—are laid out in DIN 105 (for the corresponding ASTM standards, see page 134). The DIN standards require that clinkers be free of damaging admixtures and salts, because these lead to efflorescence. DIN 1053 sets out the classification and standards for wall mortar, bonding agents, and aggregates.

Clinker dimensions and wall size
In designing clinker walls the dimensions of the bricks, governed by DIN 105–5 5 (in the U.S., ASTM C216–07a, Standard specifications for facing brick), must be taken into consideration. The standard format of a clinker is 9.4 x 4.5 x 2.7 inches (24 x 11.5 x 7.1 cm); the thin format measures 9.4 x 4.5 x 2 inches (24 x 11.5 x 5.2 cm). The standard clinker size in the U.S. is 8 x 3⅝ x 2¼ inches. There is also a diverse array of regional, historical, and manufacturer-dependent special sizes.

The measurement of the thickness, height, and length of a clinker wall depends on the brick size plus the uniform joint measurements of ½ inch (1 cm). Depending on structural and visual demands, clinkers with thicknesses of 4.5, 6.8, 9.4, 14.3, or 19.2 inches (11.5, 17.5, 24, 36.5, or 49 cm) can be used. In the U.S. the standard thicknesses are 1⅝, 2¼, 2½, 2¾, or 3⅝ inches.

Clinkers are always set with mortar joints, and they are placed according to a rigid system. The butt joints are always covered with the next row of bricks. Various systems for the alignment of bricks in a course, in combinations of *stretchers* and *headers,* produce very different appearances in the overall texture of the wall.

A stretcher is a brick laid lengthwise; the full length is visible on the wall surface. A header is laid crosswise so that only the width is visible, but its long side engages with the wall structure and stabilizes it.

Most common are *stretcher and header bonds*, but *block bonds,* where stretchers and headers alternate, are also used. In a *cross bond,* courses of stretchers and headers also alternate, but the courses of stretchers are staggered. Common decorative bonds that involve a uniform course pattern are the *Gothic bond* (staggered courses of one stretcher and one header) and the *Scotch bond* (staggered courses of two stretchers and one header). In the *Flemish bond,* different courses of stretchers and headers alternate. Depending on the alignment, either net- or diamond-shaped patterns with vertical or diagonal running lines are created in the masonry wall bond. A multitude of decorative bonding choices are available, especially when clinkers are used as facing masonry.

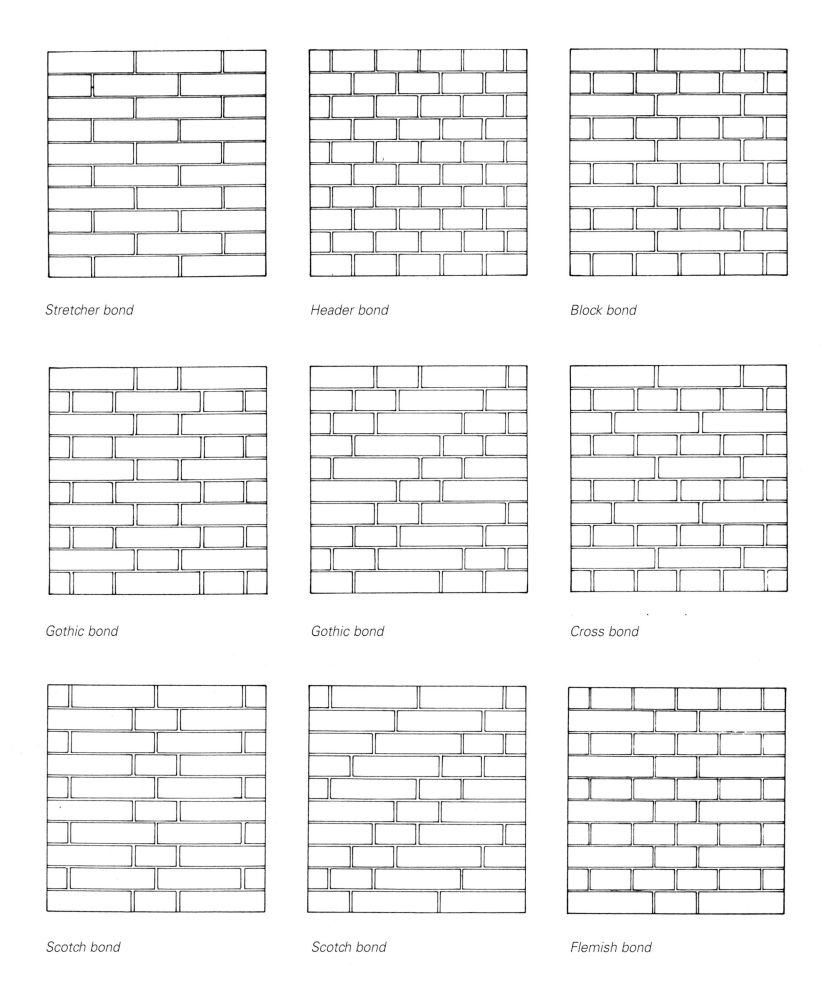

Stretcher bond

Header bond

Block bond

Gothic bond

Gothic bond

Cross bond

Scotch bond

Scotch bond

Flemish bond

Jointing

The joints of fair-faced masonry are either carefully cemented up to the upper edge or raked out 0.6 inches (1.5 cm) deep first and then jointed. Depending on the demands of the design, later jointing should be considered. To avoid efflorescence of wall and joint mortar, pozzolan cement is to be used (according to DIN 51043) In the U.S., ASTM C340–67, Specifications for Portland Pozzolan Cement; fly ash cement extender is generally used for this purpose. The best is a proven ready-made cement for clinker fair-faced masonry. The joint cement can be tinted by certain additives and sometimes pigments. The joints can either match the clinkers in color or create a contrast.

A special joint design can be achieved by filling horizontal and vertical joints differently. When the vertical joints match the clinker color and the horizontal joints create a clear contrast, the effect produced is of small horizontal ribbons that give an unusual overall appearance.

Wall base and coping

Clinker walls are rigid constructions, so they need to be solidly based and frost-resistant. Vertical expansion joints are needed at intervals of 16 to 26 feet (5–8 m). To avoid moisture, every wall of clinker or other artificial stones should include a a *horizontal dam*, usually in form of a strip of bituminized board between the base and the first brick course. Clinker masonry should not rest on the ground but be set on a concrete base.

During the construction period clinkers should be stored on wood pallets and under plastic or tarps, so that they do not become contaminated with impurities. The quantity of clinker bricks needed for a construction project must be purchased all at the same time to avoid possible color variations. To achieve a uniform coloring, clinkers are taken from different pallets at the same time so that an even mix is created and the change to a new pallet does not lead to visibe color differences.

The top of a clinker wall needs special attention. A classic execution is a *rowlock,* an upright fitted stone course. Rowlocks are beautiful, but in areas in danger of frost, they are inadvisable because of the high

Top right: Umber-colored clinker walls with rowlock harmonize with the color of the neighboring plants. Parc de Bercy, Paris, France.

Right center: Clinker walls with precast concrete coping outside a housing complex. Moabit Werder, Berlin-Mitte, Germany.

Bottom right: The waist-high supporting walls of yellowish clinker have a concrete core on which the supports of an oak pergola are based. Garden of Schloss Klessen, near Friesack, Mark Brandenburg, Germany.

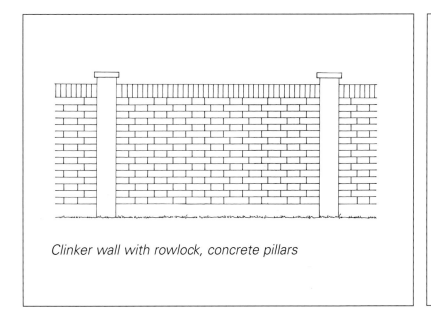

Clinker wall with rowlock, concrete pillars

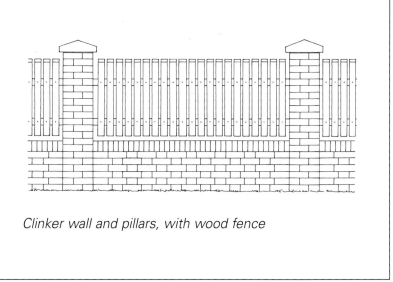

Clinker wall and pillars, with wood fence

Moabit Prison Historical Park, immediately across from Berlin's new Central Station, is a public park. The historic prison walls were restored and outfitted with a new coping of very thick plain clay roof tiles with openings at several points. The exterior walls are accentuated by pilasters; the interior walls carry inscriptions to visually reduce the enormous height and to recall the history of the place.

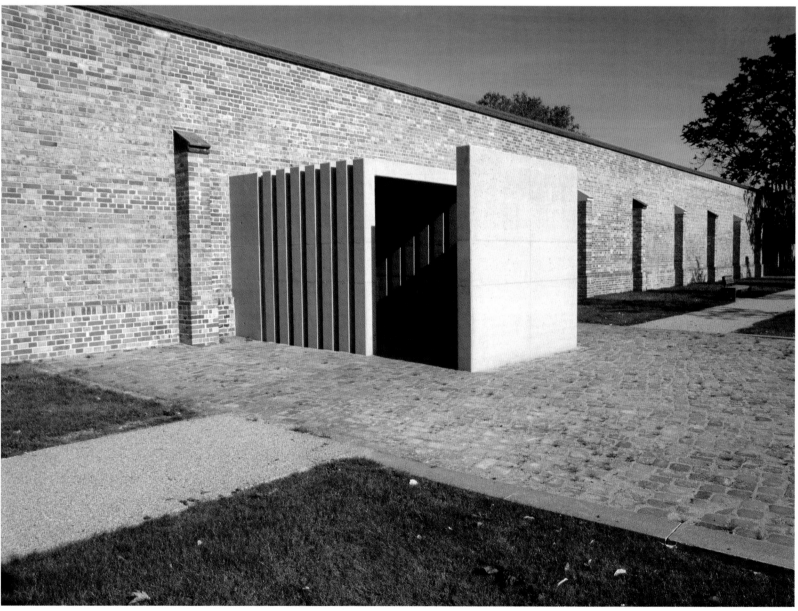

Above: Whitewashed clinker wall in a 1960s housing development in Piniehø, Denmark.

Far left: Noise insulation walls of special clinker bricks. Wilhelmina Zoological-Botanical Garden, Stuttgart.

Left: Stepped retaining wall on the waterfront on Norderney Island, in the North Sea.

number of joints. Joints are the weak links in a wall; water can penetrate them, and with frost it can produce an explosive force. But if you do decide on rowlock, build it with a slight slope, so that surface water can drain and will not pool on the top.

In Holland and England clinker walls are often covered with saddle-roof-shaped or semiround moldings, plain clay roof tile installed on a tilt, or clinkers cemented lengthwise. Often differently colored materials are used for the ceramic moldings, which creates a special allure.

Even better in terms of structural engineering, although often disdained by designers, is a pre-cast concrete coping or natural cut steel plate, or roof tiles, especially in regions with frost. Only these materials prevent water penetration effectively and guarantee that the wall structure will be free of damage for a long time.

Clinker walls in landscape planning
The beauty of a clinker wall is determined by its fine structure, the uniform size and small scale of the individual bricks, and the pleasant color of the material. In some regions, in addition to the common brick-red, red-brown, and anthracite, clinkers are available in a large palette of yellows and ochre. With their multiple design possibilities clinker walls are an appropriate design element for public outdoor spaces or home gardens. With careful selection from among the wide range of color and materials, beautiful accents can be designed.

Clinker walls are used for support,

enclosing walls, or space-creating elements, often in combination with a fence. A continuous base wall with brick pillars framing sections of wood fencing harmonizes well with of wood or steel fence elements. Pergola supports too can be of clinker masonry.

The color of the material should be chosen very carefully if the wall is to be planted later. A clinker wall that is a background for shrubs will look very different, in terms of color, than one with a hedge in the same place; this needs to be taken into consideration when planning the planting. All the shades of classic dark red bricks harmonize very well with the different greens of plants.

We can achieve playful geometric shapes with the small dimensional format of the standardized clinkers. Wedge-shaped joints can produce vertical and horizontal rolling waves without additional expensive cutting or the use of custom-made material.

Historic clinker material can be used to make beautiful walls, but there are some risks involved. Often the frost resistance of the material is not guaranteed, and the result can be damage to the masonry. Best are clinkers that were previously used as pavers in road construction; old bricks from demolished buildings are not at all suitable. The historical material often shows considerable deviations in dimension. This makes laying difficult and excludes certain masonry bonds. But the unforgettable allure of a wall made from historic clinkers can make the extra effort worthwhile.

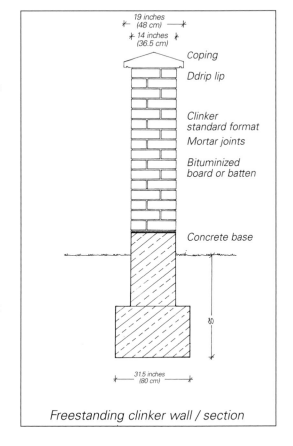

Freestanding clinker wall / section

Entrance to Parc du 26ème Centenaire, Marseille, France, built on the grounds of a former train station; the name refers to Marseille's 2,600-year history.

With the help of specially formatted brick, the acute-angled corners of this wall were rounded beautifully. Vaduz, Liechtenstein.

An anthracite clinker wall creates a border between a park-like residential area and a heavily used road. Munich-Solln, Germany.

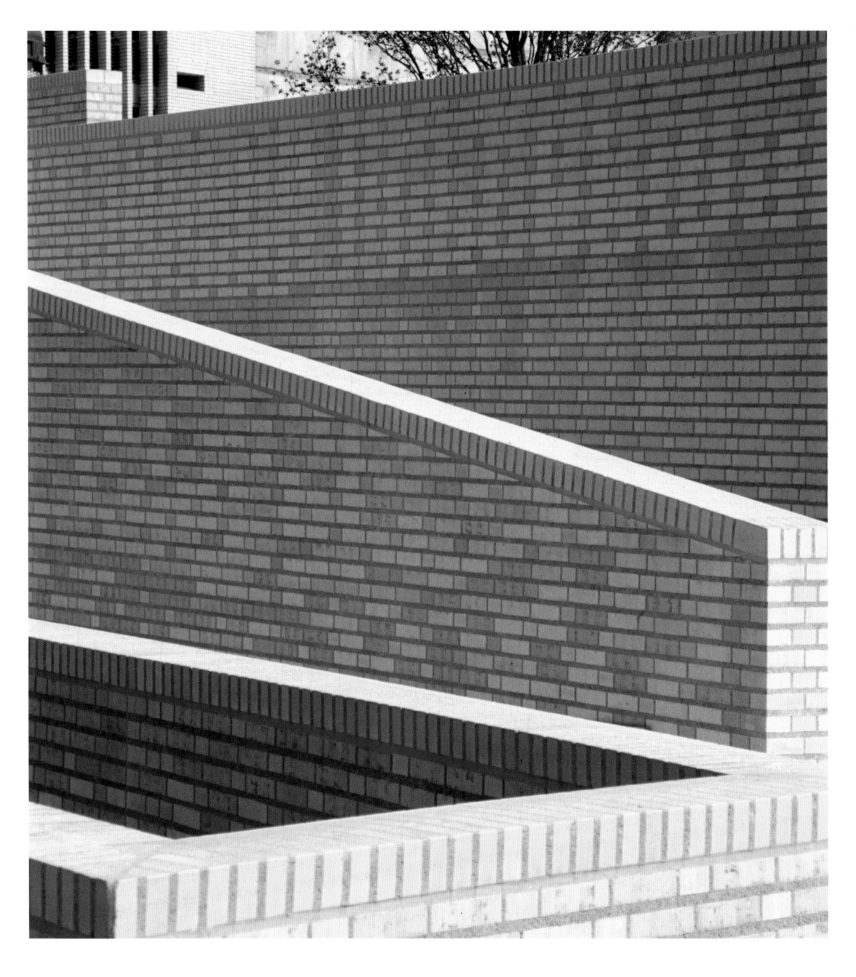

Left: Distinctive clinker walls near the new parliament building, Vaduz, Liechtenstein.

Above: The installation *Camouflaged Flowers* by Ian Hamilton Finlay consists of seven clinker walls with bronze warship silhouettes affixed to them. Within this garden, created as a *Gesamtkunstwerk*, a total work of art, there are many references to poets from Virgil to Hölderlin, and to painters from Dürer to Lorrain, along with views of a sheep meadow in an Arcadian landscape. The many lovingly arranged, delicate, and lively details of the garden give cryptic clues to the darker side of history and human existence, to war, revolution, terrorism, and violence. The machine guns, hand grenades, warships, submarines, and fighter jets, cast in bronze or carved by a stonemason, frighten and anger us. But they are not signs of a militarist's fetish; they are the artist's attempt to engage us in discourse.

Exposed masonry of sand-lime brick

Sand-lime bricks are industrially manufactured building bricks of calcium oxide (quicklime) and sand. They are pressed by machines and hardened under steam pressure at a temperature of about 392° F (200° C). DIN 106 (In the U.S., ASTM C73–05) governs the type and form of these bricks and the compression strength, bulk, and density, as well as size and shape. Sand-lime bricks are common in structural engineering and are often used in apartment buildings for partition walls because of their sound-insulating qualities. Sand-lime bricks are also well suited to outdoor walls. They are comparable to clinker bricks in their size and versatility, and they have a similar potential for creating decorative borders. With careful construction, their flat white surfaces will last beautifully for decades and will always appear fresh and modern.

Sand-lime brick masonry absorbs moisture quickly; facing away from the sun it soon gathers moss, which mars the bright appearance of the stone. The base of sand-lime brick masonry should be concrete, with a barrier course fitted between the top of the base and the bottom of the first brick masonry. The wall needs a well-functioning cover. If the strong difference in color between the stone surface and the joints is objectionable, the sand-lime brick masonry can be whitewashed and painted with mineral color.

Sand-lime bricks invites us to create relieflike designs of the wall surface because light and shadow create striking effects.

Right: Sand-lime brick masonry, Rütihof cemetery near Baden, Canton Aargau, Switzerland. The masonry is only 4.5 inches (11.5 cm) thick and is braced at the top with crosswise concrete panels and a concrete band. Following the ground level, the wall has a 10 percent decline.

Below: Sand-lime brick wall of a garden court in Karlsruhe, Germany. The wall has a concrete cover and is structured with single protruding bricks.

Sand-lime brick wall in Stäffa on Lake Zürich, in Switzerland. The stones are laid offset, creating a lively structure that is topped with a wide concrete band.

The distinct color of a plastered wall fits into the overall
color concept of the park. BUGA (National Garden Show)
2005, Munich, Germany.

Plastered walls

Plastered walls

Plastered walls are perceived as strong architectural elements. Therefore, especially near buildings, they are an appropriate medium in landscape design. Plastered walls have to be constructed with great care so that a visually pleasing and permanently damage-free appearance is guaranteed.

Plastered walls are usually erected as freestanding walls. The construction is done with artificial stones—concrete blocks, brick, sand-lime brick, or pumice stone. Often *concrete masonry units* (often called *CMUs* in the U.S.)*, which are offered by concrete manufacturers, are used. These are hollow-core blocks whose outer dimensions are generally 9 x 20 inches (24 x 50 cm), with widths of 6, 8, 10, 12, or 16 inches (15, 20, 25, 30, or 40 cm). In the U.S., CMU sizes are 4 or 8 inches high and 12 or 16 long, with available thicknesses of 2, 3, 4, 6, 8, 10, 12, and 14 inches. The most common sizes are 6 x 8 x 16, 8 x 8 x 16, and 10 x 8 x 16. The blocks are subsequently filled with poured-in-place concrete and, if necessary, reinforced with steel bars. CMUs are relatively light and can easily be used to erect walls without the formwork required for cast-in-place concrete.

Many artificial stones are not well suited for outdoor exposed masonry and therefore need to be covered with a protective layer of plaster. The plaster coating is aesthetically pleasing, but its main role is to protect the masonry beneath.

The coating can be of *single-* or *double-layer* plaster. Double-layer plaster consists of base coat and a finishing coat. Compared to the masonry the plaster is a thin coat exposed to many potential stresses and wear and tear.

Whether to plaster a concrete wall is always a difficult choice, for concrete offers different and more elaborate design possibilities, but plastering is often enough the treatment chosen. Concealing a shabby concrete surface under a coat of plaster is a fast and easy solution. The permanent, reliable bond of formed concrete and plaster can only be guaranteed with a bonding course. The concrete has to set completely before the plaster is applied. The plaster cannot be too moist.

Base and finishing coat
The plaster base coat of 0.3 to 0.6 inches (1–1.5 cm) must have sufficient elasticity that stresses can be absorbed. These stresses are created by the difference in temperature between the surface exposed to the sun and the much cooler core of the wall. Thus the plaster must be firmly fixed to the substructure. This base should be rough. If this is not possible due to the materials used, the bonding of masonry and plaster can be optimized with a *bonding course*. This is applied as a coating or done with *machine-applied plaster*. The appearance of a wall is determined to a great extent by the structure, graining, and color of the finishing coat. Depending on the execution, it will be between 0.1 and 0.3 inches (0.3–1.0 cm) thick. The various methods include *trowel-applied plaster, machine-applied plaster, stucco, rough cast render,* or *flat skimming plaster.* Unfortunately, the quality of the workmanship and the variety of textured plaster that we knew in the beginning of the twentieth century have to a large extent been lost. Rarely do we see anything else but skimming plaster today.

The finishing plaster can be purchased as white or as factory colored material. The desired color can be achieved later with a coat of silicate mineral paint. A wall as a color medium offers many possibilities for outdoor design. We can create color accents, make connections to neighboring buildings, or match the colors of other materials.

Today areas to be plastered are nearly always outfitted with plaster frames made from aluminum. These frames, standard products in the trade, are used to strip the plaster area and thereby secure a uniform plaster thickness. They are also used to even the edges. With plaster frames a higher level of precision of the plastered surfaces is achieved.

At times—for example, near landmarked buildings—we want a plaster that is more irregular than perfect. To achieve this it is better to plaster without modern aids such as plaster frames.

Base
The area at the base of a plastered wall is exposed to splashing water, so it should be done in unplastered concrete to a height

Right: The newly erected garden wall of Grosspertholz Palace near Gmünd, Austria, has a single-pitch-roof cover topped with plain tiles and closing crest tiles.

Below: The plastered garden wall on the south side of the Schwetzingen Palace Gardens also has a single-pitch-roof top, covered with regular plain clay roof tiles of a different shape.

of at least 8 inches (20 cm). Where this is not possible or desirable, a special water resistant plaster should be used. This plaster, separated from the wall area above by a *plaster reveal,* is a firm cement plaster that absorbs almost no moisture. It is not very elastic, however, and therefore is not suitable for plastering the entire wall area. It is essential to put a horizontal damp-proof barrier such as a layer of bituminized board between the base and the completed wall, so that rising moisture is suppressed.

A plastered wall should, if possible, have a vertical layer of *gravel drainage* behind the entire wall. It should be about 16 inches (40 cm) wide and extend to the foundation. Rain water will be drained off and cannot be soaked up by capillary action. The base drainage area should be sloped so that condensation is quickly diverted away from the wall.

Crown
In temperate and northern climates, walls with plastered tops always need a solid cap. Only frost-free southern climates, where less precipitation accumulates, can do without it. The cover protects the masonry from penetrating moisture. A horizontal overhang of about 1 inch (3 cm) and a correctly executed weather groove underneath it prevent water from flowing across the wall and creating ugly streaks.

In the past, wall covers were constructed in structurally advantageous ways, usually with roof tiles. Today this type of construction is usually reserved for walls near historic buildings. Most often plain clay roof tiles are used. It is best to mount them on a batten that is fastened to the slanted wall top, and then to solidify them at the edges. Depending on the thickness of the wall, three or four rows of roof tile covers are topped with a plain semiround ridge tile.

Today, special concrete or stone masonry caps or copings with saddle-roof-shaped cross sections are used to top plastered walls. Because these cover units are limited in length, they require butt joints at regular intervals. These joints are the weak link of all wall tops done with cover stones; the mortar often does not seal the joints permanently, allowing water to penetrate and permeate the plaster below the joint. Spots develop and the frost causes chips, but by fitting a small chamfer in form of a V-shaped bent sheet-metal strip or a semiround plastic channel directly below the cover, water penetration can be prevented simply and unobtrusively.

The best way to achieve a permanent, undamaged plastered wall, however, is to use a professionally made steel plate cover. Steel manufacturers understand the thermal behavior of steel plate in the shape of expansion joints. After steel, a zinc or aluminum plate is preferable over copper because water dripping down from copperplate often leaves traces of verdigris on the wall surface.

A cover of galvanized steel, possibly lacquered or coated with stove enamel, is another choice. These plates are sized so that joints occur at intervals of a maximum of 20 feet (6 m). Just as with sheet metal, we also have to consider thermal expansion with steel plates. If the plates are spliced with pressed joints that do not allow expansion, they are a weak link through which water will penetrate. To avoid this, and to create an appealing open joint, a workable solution is staggered splices for the entire length of a hard rubber strip; alternatively, a small chamfer built in below the splicing will keep water out.

Causes of cracking
Plastered walls are rigid structures. They need a foundation that extends below the frost line. To avoid cracks, continuous expansion joints should be installed at regular intervals as predetermined breaking points or zones. Cracks make plastered walls unsightly and no client will tolerate them.

Cracks may be structural or restricted to the plaster or plaster prime coat. Structural cracks usually result from a faulty foundation, the lack of expansion joints, or incomplete expansion joints that do not run continuously from base to top. Cracks can also be caused by a change of material in the masonry, such as a change from brick to concrete. Such cracks can be prevented by building a plaster reinforcement in the form of expanded metal or fiberglass mats.

Above top: A thin, precise cap of galvanized steel plate. Stuttgart-Bad Cannstatt, Germany.

Above: Plastered wall with a zinc sheet cap executed with expansion joints at intervals of 16 feet (5 m). Copenhagen, Denmark.

Left: Base, cover, and edging all of concrete in a free-standing wall of colored plaster. Waterford Museum of Treasures, Waterford, Ireland.

A concrete retaining wall covered with steel plates 0.3 inches (0.8 cm) thick. Plaça Vila de Madrid, Barcelona, Spain.

Walls with facings

Walls with facings

There are good reasons to face walls with materials other than stone masonry, which might seem too colorless, expensive, or traditional. If plastering seems too ordinary and too fragile, sometimes a facing is an alternative. Wall facings always aim for an uncommon, distinctive appearance, and are the finish of choice for the division and structuring of rather large wall spaces.

The Jardin Atlantique, an avant-garde roof-garden park 60 feet (18 m) above the Maine-Montparnasse TGV station in the center of Paris, boasts remarkable examples of faced concrete walls. The compound's 8.4 acres (3.4 ha), designed by François Brun, Michael Péna, and Christine Schnitzler, were completed in 1994. Both the basic concept— building a public park above a train station— and the many details are stimulating, in particular the design of the walls that separate the various functions of the park.

One of the concrete walls is covered with polygonal natural stone plates, not in tight joint design, a form familiar to us, but like a crazy quilt of single screwed-on plates. The ends of the bolts don't mask the facing; rather they emphasize the cover's function and make it visible.

Elsewhere in the park, marking the borders of a playground, are concrete walls, 10 feet (3 m) high, covered with mosaics of broken tiles. These blue and green walls are reminiscent of the mosaics in the Parc Güell by Antoni Gaudí (1852–1926), which date from 1900–1914. This 42-acre (17-ha) park near the center of Barcelona was named a UNESCO World Heritage site in 1984. It is special not only because of the clever overall concept, but also because the material for its imaginative wall facings came from the waste of a nearby tile factory.

Steel

Recently garden and landscape designers have discovered steel. More and more, galvanized and varnished or raw and rusting steel plates are used in designing outdoor spaces. Steel, with supports of up to 24 inches (60 cm) in height and corresponding thickness, an L-shaped cross section, and possibly a welded-on reinforcing rib, can fulfill all the functions of a supporting wall.

Walls covered with 0.5-inch (1.5- cm) thick rusting steel plates. Spreebogenpark, Berlin, Germany.

For higher and longer walls, it is more economical and more structurally sound to use a conventional concrete wall and cover it with steel plate or steel panels.

In Barcelona's Botanical Garden, designed by Bet Figueras and Carlos Ferrater and completed in 1999, the rather high supporting walls were covered with raw steel plate, developing a characteristic style element for the entire complex. The project was very influential, and soon wall facings of rusting steel became internationally fashionable. Steel plate facing was also used in the 15-acre (6-ha) Berlin Spreebogenpark (completed in 2005) designed by the Swiss architects

Right: Rough natural stone slabs were mounted on the concrete wall with visible bolt heads. The blue tiles of the mosaic facing (bottom) give the enclosure of a playground an original, buoyant tone. Both are at the Jardin Atlantique, Paris.

Weber and Sauer. The center axis of the park, running north–south, 66 feet (20 m) wide and 328 feet (100 m) long, is enclosed on both sides by concrete walls that are faced with steel plates 0.5 inches (1.5 cm) thick. In the upper part the steel plates are doubled to create a 3-inch (8-cm) parapet that prevents the wall from caving in. There are wall facings of rusting steel in other parts of Berlin's Spreebogenpark. The corroding surfaces are fragile. We can easily apply lettering or cut into them; this will not look like damage, but like signs of use. One advantage is that the rusty surfaces are not inviting to graffiti artists: the steel plates have been graffiti free; on the other hand, unfortunately, an ugly white bloom appears at the joints.

Glass

Glass has gained importance as a building material in the last twenty years in all areas of architecture and construction. Cost-effective laminated glass and technically advanced, elegant bracket systems allow glass to be fastened securely and permanently without frame construction. Glass is often used for balconies, railings, and even floor coverings. By code, *safety glass,* which does not cause injury when it breaks, is always employed. It generally consists of two or three glass panels with PVC interlayers; it is usually white-green. Laminated safety glass panels can also be used for wall facing. Glass does not develop a patina; it retains a perfect surface as long as it is cleaned regularly. Because of light reflections, glass surfaces are always light and elegant, even in areas with little light. Glass as an architectural

element has a strong effect and is therefore only appropriate near buildings.

Wood

Very simple and obvious but rarely seen is the facing of an unattractive wall with

The side walls of a sunken court are covered with frosted glass and steel plate. Kunstakademie Stuttgart (Art Academy of Stuttgart), Germany.

wood slats, latticework, or trelliswork for climbing plants. Often such a treatment is not designed to help plants climb, but rather to give character to the wall's surface. The lifespan of wood facing is limited unless it is protected from the weather.

Walls covered with wooden slats may allow

The stringer is faced in the same way as the base wall and garage door, with glazed wooden slats. Cologne-Marienburg, Germany

design interplay with other outdoor elements such as fences, gates, or a building's shutters. Wood is suitable for coloration with either opaque paint or semitransparent glaze. Wood that has been colored is striking, but needs more maintenance and periodic repainting or restaining.

Plants

A common method of hiding wall surfaces is to plant them, usually with climbing plants that grow upward on the wall with anchoring roots or adhesive discs. As noted earlier, ivy (*Hedera helix*) and Virginia creeper (*Parthenocissus quinquefolia*) are the most popular and suitable climbers. Ivy has advantage of being evergreen. After a few years, however, it grows thick and has to be cut back. Virginia creeper has no leaves in the winter, but for two to three weeks in the fall it has beautiful color; overall it is more disciplined than ivy. Ivy and Virginia creeper can be combined handsomely and will be beautiful for a few years. The Virginia creeper grows faster in the beginning, but it will eventually be displaced by the ivy.

The anchoring roots of ivy and Virginia creeper leave traces on the walls they grow on. They don't cause damage, but the marks are very hard to remove. Thus it is a good idea to use climbers that can be grown with the aid of bracing wire, steel trellises, or lattices, such as roses, wisteria, clematis, Dutchman's pipe, and many other plants. The framework limits the space available for the plants and prevents them from spreading uncontrollably.

Hedges

Plants, rocks, and often water are the most important elements in garden design. The emphasis should always be on the plants, the design with greenery. Too much stone can create a feeling of lifelessness and sadness, so covered areas, supporting walls, and stairs should not look too massive or be a garden's dominant element.

In creating spaces and planning structures, we need to balance hedge and wall; in planning the topography we need to balance slope and retaining wall. Often a hedge doesn't feel secure enough as a border; perhaps a slope can't be created because of space limitations or because it seems, from a design standpoint, too soft and not a precise enough contour.

Convincing green solutions can be created by combining walls and hedges. A wall can be faced entirely with trimmed hedges, and designed without any aesthetic considerations in concrete or prefabricated masonry panels. Such a wall functions as a background; it is visually unimportant because the hedge masks it.

Enclosing walls too can be faced with hedges for their entire height. Sometimes high walls are needed for security reasons. To break the visual expanse, the hedges might only be used for part of the wall's height; the resulting difference reduces the perceived height by creating interesting interplay of wall and hedge, stone and greenery. In a variation, a wall can be combined with large shrubs or trees, for example lindens. This way, enclosures more than 20 feet (6 m) can, despite their height, appear pleasant.

Any hedges that are commercially available are suitable for facing. Most impressive are evergreens like yew (*Taxus baccata*) and boxwoods (*Buxus sempervirens*). European beeches (*Fagus sylvatica*) retain their copper-colored fall foliage in winter and provide a permanent screen from view. American beeches (*Fagus grandifolia*) have a similar character with a golden fall color, but are green all spring and summer.

The possibility of later hedge planting should be considered during wall construction. Proper plant growth conditions are important: a hedge needs to have enough root space. The foundation shouldn't overhang too much; if necessary an *L-shaped foundation* should be used. When using wall panels it is important that the foundation wedges don't reach too far into the root area. Excess concrete and other material residues have to be removed carefully before filling the excavations. Compacted ground must be decompacted and aerated. With heavy, cohesive ground, a 6-inch (15-cm) layer of chips, 20 to 24 inches (50–60 cm) deep, can be fitted for drainage to prevent waterlogging that might kill newly planted hedges.

Right center: Concrete wall with Virginia creepers. Banks of the Spree River Berlin-Mitte, Germany.

Right middle: Concrete wall with wood posts and tensioning rope to hold plantings. Rolle, Lake Geneva, Switzerland.

Right bottom: Concrete wall covered with ivy and Virginia creeper, and a painted and artistically designed wall panel at a right angle, enfold a small seating area. House garden, Ettlingen-Oberweier, Germany.

Gabion-faced concrete walls at the Scottish parliament,
Edinburgh, Scotland.

Gabions

Gabions

For some years gabions have been a common sight in landscape design. Gabions are used in road construction and slope protection and, more and more, in challenging garden and landscape design. They offer a multitude of design opportunities.

The word *gabion* comes from the Italian *gabbia* (cage, basket). It refers to a wire mesh filled with stones that is used to create wall-like structures, waterside slopes, or freestanding walls. Prefabricated cages of galvanized mesh wire or custom-made stainless steel wire mesh are 3 to 6 feet (1–2 m) long, 2 to 2.5 feet (80–100 cm) deep, and 1.5 to 2 feet (50–80 cm) high. Many manufacturers also offer custom-made products.

Filling

The mesh size depends on the type and dimensions of the designated filling. Gabions may be purchased as prefilled construction elements or be filled on location with suitable stone material. This could be rough stone, irregular setts, gravel, or rough gravel.

To meet high design standards, the exposed surfaces can be arranged carefully and professionally, wall-fashion, and then backfilled with ballast. We can design the exposed areas with select stone masonry material and create a connection to the other natural stone used in associated structures like stairs or floors. To economize, the backfilling can be done with locally available material. The gabions on the outdoor grounds of the new parliament building in Edinburgh, filled with old stone masonry fragments, are very appealing.

Filled gabions are moved with a truck-mounted crane, so erecting them is fast and effective. With construction sites that are very difficult to reach, the fill material is transported to the site in small amounts, or it may be extracted on site and the gabion filled there. This is laborious, but at times it is the only possibility for erecting a retaining wall.

Advantages and disadvantages

Originally gabions were used primarily to secure slopes in road construction, especially at the foot of slopes where rocks were in danger of falling because of waterlogging and slope water. A decade ago, architects discovered the high design potential of gabions. Since then, they have been used more and more in garden construction and landscaping and in designing landscapes. Depending on the filling, the gabions offer a varied surface structure with a natural appearance similar to rough stone. We can create strong regional connections with the stones we use; moreover, gabions can be integrated very well near rocks and do not look like foreign material. Gabions, like dry-placed walls, have a high ecological value; they offer living space to many animals.

Another advantage is simple and cost-effective construction. In hard-to-reach areas—for example, securing slopes in the mountains, creating gardens in inaccessible spots, or building row-houses on a slope—gabions can be erected without a lot of construction machinery. They should be filled on site with the stone material. Gabions are elastic and water-permeable and do not need an extensive foundation or drainage. They are placed on a stable, water-diverting foundation with a slight batter toward the slope, usually on a simple base of broken stones. With multilayered, higher gabion walls, the single cages are filled stairlike, one above another. For more security they can be connected to each other.

Among the disadvantage of gabions is the

Above: The gabions are planted with *Clematis montana* 'Rubens'; the wires of the gabion cages furnish the ideal climbing help. Ettlingen, Germany.

Right: Gabion filled with river pebbles.

Far right: With a solid coping, a small gabion wall becomes a strongly designed wall.

need for a lot of space because of the high installation depth, the very heavy weight, and the enormous amount of material needed. The construction of gabions is only advisable when the site can be reached without problem by transportation vehicles or if suitable material for filling is available on location.

Design of exposed surfaces

Next to the careful wall-like layering of chosen, color-coordinated natural stone material, the exposed surfaces of gabions can also be designed for visual interest; filling them with different materials creates beautiful color and structural effects. Staggering the size of the construction materials creates a pleasing appearance. Here, we need to pay close attention to adjusting the material size and mesh size of the gabions.

Aside from different natural stone materials, the gabions can be filed with stacked bricks or recycled materials. There are no limits to the imagination, although we need to keep in mind that the overall appearance shouldn't be too disquieting or wild. With professional installation gabions last a long time. We should avoid designing permanent structures according to fashion trends.

For short-lived installations like show gardens or garden expositions, gabions can be used for inventive designs and filled with time-limited, perishable materials such as wood or brushwood.

Applications

Gabions of just 12 to 20 inches (30–50 cm) in depth can be purchased for freestanding walls for house gardens. The relatively simple installation and the easy foundation make this type of enclosure much more cost-effective than a comparable wall of poured-in-place concrete.

Today gabions are also often used to line riverbanks or for projects designed along the water's edge. Because they can easily be placed in water and can be filled on location, gabions have clear advantages over other construction methods. To withstand the demanding environment, especially in zones of alternating water currents, the wire used in and around the water should be significantly thicker.

Gabions can be covered with large-sized stone masonry caps, which give them a handsome appearance. Adding a wood cover to create a seating area is also a possibility.

Planted gabions

As noted, the mesh wire of gabions offers first-rate possibilities for climbing plants. Without additional aids we can achieve an intense greening of the gabions so long as we can plant at the foot of the construction. The wire offers support for the plants, and even high gabions are quickly overgrown. Next to ivy and Virginia creeper, wild clematis (and other clematis species) have proved themselves good choices. If it is not possible to plant at the foot of the gabion, the planting can also be done from the top of the wall, although since climbing plants grow upward small corrections may be necessary. Alternately, hanging shrubs like winter jasmine (*Jasminum nudiflorum*), bush clover (*Lespedeza thunbergii*), or wild roses can be used.

There are also completely green gabions created by systematic inlay of osier stakes (live willow stakes) when the wall is erected. As long as there is contact with the ground on the back side, the stakes will root and flower, so that soon the stones are covered with a green veil. To avoid too lush vegetation or too much growth away from the wall, occasionally cutting back the stakes to rejuvenate them is recommended.

Gabions can be completely filled with soil instead of stones: a landscape cloth prevents the soil from trickling out. Soil gabions are not filled until after the installation work is finished. Then the fabric is cut in spots and plants placed there. Successful plantings depend on continuous artificial watering; very little rain reaches the vertical plant areas, and gabions that face south dry out very quickly.

Right: The wall of a viewing platform in Loffenau in the northern Black Forest is made from gabions filled with northern Black Forest granite.

The Rotary Park, a walkable gabion sculpture by the Danish artist Olafur Eliasson. The sculpture is 13 feet (4 m) high and has a diameter of 33 feet (10 m). It is one of a total of sixty art objects that have been installed on the 82-mile *Kunstwegen* sculpture road between the Dutch town of Zwolle and the German town Nordhorn.

Right: Wall of a well made of gabions with carefully staggered filling of color-contrasting natural stone material. Landesgartenschau (State Garden Show), 2004, Wolfsburg, Germany

Below: Gabions used for shoreline stabilization. Parc Diagonal Mar, Barcelona, Spain.

Below right: Gabions cover concrete walls at the new Scottish parliament. The gabion cages are made from stainless steel and are filled with cut stones generated from demolition operations at the site. Edinburgh, Scotland

Cemetery wall of rammed earth; Wil,
Canton St. Gallen, Switzerland

Rammed earth walls

Rammed earth walls

Earth is one of the world's oldest building materials, used in ancient cultures. It is still very important today in many African and Asian countries with hot and dry climates . More than one-third of the world's population lives in houses that are partly or entirely built from earth. The earth is either processed into air-dried bricks of suitable measurements or is rammed into the desired shape. In this type of construction the moist earth material is inserted into a casing in layers of about 6 inches (15 cm). Then it is compacted to about two-thirds of the filling height by ramming. Most of the time, after the removal of the casing, walls are not plastered, faced, or finished in any way. Their appeal lies in their archaic beauty. The famous Berber settlements in Morocco, the fairy-tale-like architecture of Yemen, and large parts of the Great Wall of China are built of rammed earth.

Earth as a building material

Soil is the product of change; it is created when stones disintegrate and it consists mainly of sand and clay. We find loam everywhere on earth as loess clay, immediately under the humus layer of the ground, or as boulder clay washed up in meadows.

No two soils are alike; the mix of sand, clay, added ballast chips, and gravel varies greatly. Therefore it has different characteristics as far as structural engineering is concerned. All naturally available soils that are mixed with gravel are well suited for rammed earth construction.

The simple, unadorned texture of soil and its extraordinary insulating properties have led to a new appreciation of this building material in industrialized nations. Soil is available everywhere. It is easily processed. The industry that specializes in ecological construction materials offers optimized, color-coordinated ready mixes for rammed earth construction. The material arrives at the site in big bags, ready to be processed.

An important disadvantage of all construction with soil is the solubility of the material even after it hardens. Driving rain and splash water cause damage through runlets; heavy downpours and frost can cause huge damage to wet wall surfaces. For this reason, earth walls have been of secondary importance in European and American building history. However, a structurally sound execution, especially of the base and top, can contain the erosion problems. This way, in our climates too, we can guarantee the longevity of earth walls.

Garden walls of rammed earth

Several years ago artists and landscape architects discovered rammed earth construction anew. They found a fascinating design element in the naturalness of the material and its incomparable expressiveness. The fine, almost graphic traces of processing and the natural color play give these walls their tremendous allure. The color scale encompasses all earth tones, from beige to ochre, gray to brown, and beautiful opaque reds. The mineral pigments are light-resistant, so the colors do not fade. The material doesn't have to be enhanced by a facing or a coat of paint; it appeals is through the basic material—its vivid structure, color, and texture.

The possibility of extracting and processing the material on location is very attractive, and not only to ecologically minded customers. In an ideal scenario, the excavated material from below the humus layer can be used right away for the erection of a garden wall.

Kienast, Vogt and Partner, a Swiss firm that specializes in garden and landscape architecture, were leaders in the development of new compacted earth walls. They executed several projects, most often in cooperation with the Austrian artist Martin Rauch. Rauch is considered a pioneer of temporary rammed earth construction. In his own words, he is not about "dull, dilettante retro-style," but about the renewal of an old, ecologically sound construction technique. In cooperation with several architects and garden and landscape architects he has realized many large projects, including interior walls in buildings and the enclosing walls of sophisticated private gardens and cemeteries. Among his works are the cemetery walls in Wil near St. Gallen in Switzerland, the cemetery walls and chapel in Batschuns, Voralberg, Austria, and several works in the village of St. Gerold in the Grosse Walsertal (Great Walser Valley), also in Voralberg, Austria. Here, in 1994, a common tomb wall 230 feet (70 m) long and 6 feet (2 m) high was built of rammed earth. It is outfitted with uniform nameplates and protected at the top with clinker slabs.

Right: Cemetery wall of rammed earth with Cor-Ten steel cover. A small gutter is installed under the joints of the cover plates.

The symbolic significance of the ephemeral and recyclable building material is especially important for this tomb.

The best-known of Martin Rauch's projects is the Chapel of Reconciliation in what was formerly known as the infamous "death strip" of the Berlin Wall. The rammed earth wall in the small sanctuary was made of locally found loam earth mixed with brick fragments from the small church that stood there earlier but had been destroyed during the era of the German Democratic Republic. The Chapel of Reconciliation is a work of high aesthetic value, with subtle references to place and history.

Martin Rauch not only perfected the material mix—usually 50 to 60 percent earth with additives such as broken bricks, lava, or chips, or with fiber materials such as flax or straw—but he also developed contemporary ways of processing it. The mixture applied to the casing is compacted with electric and pneumatic rammers, or for the appropriate wall size with vibration rollers, sometimes called slab rollers. As a rule, modern casing systems that are common for building with concrete are used. Additional reinforcements are needed with machine compaction methods because of the tremendous force applied to the casing. For some projects Rauch used elements of rammed earth that had been prefabricated in the workshop.

Construction details

Walls of rammed earth construction are usually enormously thick because the casing for compacting has to be walkable and fit for traffic. This results in measurements of 16 to 24 inches (40–60 cm), an advantage for outdoor walls because slight erosion is easily absorbed by walls of these dimensions. The overall appearance and stability are not compromised.

An earth wall can be stripped from the formwork immediately after compaction. Drying time is five to eight weeks, depending on wall size, temperature, and humidity. The dried earth weighs 1.8 to 2.2 metric tons per cubic yard and has a residual moisture of about 6 to 7 percent.

Erosion damage can be averted with the help of careful processing. Cement-containing courses inserted at regular intervals will lessen erosion damage considerably, although some of the naturalness of the material is lost. Optimal solutions have to be found for each project. Larger stones are advantageous; they are anchored firmly inside the wall and function as erosion brakes.

The best erosion protection is achieved when layers of stone or brick are inserted at regular intervals into the casing. Wooden boards are then fitted horizontally between the outer edges of the brick or stone layers; when the casing is compressed, the layers of earth are pushed back to the depth of the board. The result, when the boards are removed, is that the earth layers are recessed back from the leading edges of the brick or stone layers (see picture at center right), and so protected from the weather. The result is a banded surface structure, clearly different from flat formed loam walls. This type of rammed earth construction is used primarily for building outside walls, where reliable erosion protection is especially needed.

The foundation and base of a rammed earth wall are often done in concrete or stone masonry to a height of 12 inches (30 cm) in order to protect from splash water damage. To avoid rising dampness, a horizontal barrier in the form of bitumen sheeting should to be inserted between the base and the earth courses of the wall.

An earth wall must have a waterproof cap with ample overhang and a weather groove. Zinc, copper sheet, steel, ceramic, concrete, or stone masonry slabs are appropriate choices. For the rammed earth walls of the Wil cemetery, semiround chamfers that resemble a water spout in function and appearance were inserted between the joints of the steel plate covers. This detail guarantees that no water will penetrate at the joints. It also looks good.

The natural aging of earth walls is fascinating. Minor damage is not considered a defect. If necessary, however, damaged areas can be restored. The unlimited recyclability of earth is unique among all building materials. Adding large amounts of water makes even hardened earth kneadable and plastic, a simple recycling method that allows the optimum use of resources. Sophisticated designs are possible, and the construction technique fosters a deep connection to the site of the project.

Above: Cemetery wall at Provost's Church, St. Gerold, Grosses Walsertal (Great Walser Valley), Austria.

Right top: Enclosing wall of a village cemetery. Batschuns, Vorarlberg, Austria.

Right center: Flat bricks inserted in regular courses create an attractive surface structure and provide additional erosion protection.

Right bottom: Rammed earth wall as the boundary of a private garden. The excavation material from the construction of the building was used to build the wall. Maur/Grafensee, Zürich Canton, Switzerland.

Wall of recycled material in Ziegleipark
(Brickworks Park), Heidbronn, Germany.

Walls of recycled
and similar materials

Walls of recycled and similar materials

Walls of recycled material are original and authentic. The execution demands imagination and sure instinct on the part of the mason to achieve a convincing overall appearance. In a suitable environment the interplay with the vegetation can be quite poetic. However, we must use construction methods that are sound and farsighted. We need to consider whether the individual materials are suitable for wall construction and whether frost resistance can be guaranteed if that is a consideration. In particular, suitability and frost resistance should be considered with materials that have been used in a very different context, for example, for partitions inside buildings.

It is not uncommon to reuse materials. Materials from different building periods and different contexts have been used for many historic buildings. Since the 1990s designs have been developed with recycled materials that make use of the effects of transmutation. Strange, colorful, collagelike masonry images have been created with very different materials. Walls from recycled materials are, depending on their composition and the size of the individual parts, stacked as dry-placed walls or bricked up with mortar like stone masonry.

Like the recycled broken stone that is now the standard choice for road-building, walls of recycled material are the result of ecological considerations and the search for alternative, resource-conserving techniques. These unusual solutions were prompted by the desire to reuse materials on location, as well as to avoid lengthy transport routes for the removal of the old and delivery of the new.

Walls of recycled materials demand intensive cooperation between designer and builder. We can plan the contours and measurements of the wall, but we may not know what its final appearance will be. It is strongly advisable to create samples. Walls of recycled materials often display lively contrasts, unusual colors, and interesting, varied structures. They are especially appealing when we can recognize individual materials in the masonry: ridge tiles, drainpipes, concrete slabs, or entire chunks of old brick masonry. These details tell their strange, unique stories. Yet we often walk a tightrope with recycled walls: either they are a resourceful resurrection or embarrassing, tacky bricolage. A perfect cover or a strong formal enclosure help to avoid the impression of a chaotic mix of materials, but most important of all is a design appropriate to the neighboring areas.

Often the material for recycled walls is free. Either it is a collection of individual scavenged elements or material amassed on location as a result of demolition. Remnants from the stone masonry trade, from quarries, or from stonemasons' operations can be used.

Brickworks Park

A striking example of a wall of recycled materials is the Ziegeleipark (Brickworks Park) in Heilbronn-Böckingen, Germany, designed by Karl Bauer and Jörg Stötzer. On the 104 acres (42 ha) of this derelict industrial site, an appealing, eventful natural space, a public theme park that all generations delight in, was built. Despite the new planning and renovation, the historic background—the memory of clay pit and brickyard times—is still present.

The place gains its special identity from a cleverly orchestrated program of "preserving the evidence." It was a bold decision to reuse all of the demolition materials found on the site, such as using recycled broken stone for foundations and dry-placed walls. Even the old railroad tracks, with their beautiful and recognizable solid steel sections, were used to enclose the paths. All these seemingly useless objects develop remarkable poetic qualities in recycling. Here, at the site, the results feel harmonious.

One of the main characteristics of the Brickworks Park is the 164-foot (50-m) high edge of the clay pit that forms the eastern border of the complex. After mining stopped, many insect and bird species settled here, many of them on the list of endangered species. The earth walls were

Top: A remarkable example of a wall made from recycling materials is found in the *Ziegeleipark* (Brickworks Park). The dry-placed wall that confines a protecting strip in front of the landmarked earth wall is entirely made of demolition materials found in the compound.

Bottom: Inventive design for a wall from recycled materials in a house garden near Bern, Switzerland.

declared a natural landmark in 1991. The 164-foot (50-m) wide strip with its natural, wild vegetation and rolling dry-placed wall, almost 3 feet (1 m) high, made of recycled materials, is clearly different from the neighboring meadows. A protected zone fronts the natural landmark. One cannot imagine a more suitable choice than recycled material
for this place. Unfortunately, after a few years the walls were vandalized, and some of the materials were insufficiently frost resistant, so many areas showed damage.

Walls of firewood and other materials

The use of stacked firewood as a space demarcation is not unusual and has a long tradition in rural communities. The Danish garden architect Sven Ingvar Andersson

(1927–2007) was the first to take up this idea and introduce it as a style element in garden design. For an exhibition garden in Stockholm in 1986 he built a dividing wall of logs 9 feet (3 m) high and 30 feet (10 m) long. Single logs projected out at intervals of 4 feet (1.25 m) to create a bench of continuous slim bamboo sections. This project was widely publicized and became a model for others.

If the stacked firewood lacks a solid cover and is exposed to the elements, the wood will soon look ugly. Without ventilation, it will rot within a few years. If a permanent solution is desired, the lowest wood layer should be placed at least 6 inches (15 cm) above the ground by laying the logs on concrete sleepers. The wall sections should not exceed 10 feet (3 m) in length, and they should be precisely framed at each intersection to achieve an aesthetically

pleasing result. Steel frames are a good choice for this purpose because of their longer durability.

Apart from firewood there are countless other easily stackable materials for building walls and boundaries. At the National Garden Festival in Jülich, Germany, in 1998, a landscape was created with tightly bundled recycled paper. For the 2000 Garden Festival, at Ippenburg Castle in Bad Essen, Germany, the firm of Klahn, Singer, and Partners experimented with bales of straw. Glass bottles, beverage cases, wooden pallets, pressed scrap metal, and many other inexpensive and standardized elements have been used to construct walls and barriers. For temporary boundaries needed in exhibitions, these materials might be suitable and original, but for regular use in garden design and landscaping they are not appropriate.

Right: With careful coursing and precise gradation of the cross-section dimensions, normal fire wood becomes an artistic installation a temporary wall. BUGA (National Garden Show) 2001, Potsdam, Germany.

Standards for walls

Abbreviations
ACI: American Concrete Institute
ASCE: American Society of Civil Engineers
ASTM: American Standards for Testing and
    Materials
CSI: Construction Specifications Institute
IBC: International Building Code

DIN 105 Unit masonry standards
ASTM C216-07a Standard Specification
    for Facing Brick (Solid Masonry Units
    Made from Clay or Shale)
ASTM F1312-90 (2007) Standard
    Specification for Brick, Insulating, High
    Temperature, Fire Clay
ASTM C119-08e1 Standard Terminology
    Relating to Dimension Stone
ASTM C119-06 Standard Terminology
    Relating to Dimension Stone (Historical
    Standard)

DIN 106 Sand-lime-brick standards
ASTM C73-05 Standard Specification for
    Calcium Silicate Brick (Sand-Lime
    Brick)

DIN 1045 Concrete bearing structures
In the United States structural standards
    are regulated in local building codes.
    Refer to ACI 318-08 Building Code
    requirements for structural concrete.

ASTM C125-09 Standard Terminology relating
    to concrete and concrete aggregates

ASTM C294-05 Standard Descriptive
    Nomenclature for Constituents of
    Concrete Aggregates

DIN 1048 Test procedures for concrete
ASTM C1077-09b Standard Practice for
    Laboratories Testing Concrete and
    Concrete Aggregates for Use in
    Construction and Criteria for Laboratory
    Evaluation

ASTM C94 / C94M-09a Standard
    Specification for Ready-Mixed
    Concrete

DIN 1053 Masonry standards
ASTM WK52 New Practice for Unit Masonry
    Workmanship

Structural design follows local building
    codes. IBC Section 2103 is widely
    used in the United States.

ACI 530.1/ASCE 6/TMS 602
ASTM C1232-10 Standard Terminology of
    Masonry
ASTM C476-09 Standard Specification for
    Grout for Masonry

DIN 1054 Subsoil, allowable load on subsoil
IBC Chapter 18

ASTM D5878-05 Standard Guide for Using
    Rock Mass Classification Systems for
    Engineering Purposes
ASTM D2487-06e1 Standard Practice for
    Classification of Soils for Engineering
    Purposes (Unified Soil Classification
    System)
ASTM D2488-09a Standard Practice for
    Description and Identification of Soils
    (Visual-Manual Procedure)

DIN 1055 Design load, superimposed load
    on structural elements.
ASCE/SEI 7-05   Minimum Design
    Loads for Buildings and Other
    Structures

DIN 1069 Earth structures (eliminated
    without substitution in 1971)
ASTM E2392 - 05 Standard Guide for Design
    of Earthen Wall Building Systems

DIN 1964 Plaster and stucco work
ASTM C932-06 Standard Specification for
    Surface-Applied Bonding Compounds
    for Exterior Plastering

ASTM C897-05 (2009) Standard
    Specification for Aggregate for Job-
    Mixed Portland Cement-Based Plasters

ASTM C1032-06 Standard Specification for
    Woven Wire Plaster Base

ASTM C587-04 Standard Specification for
    Gypsum Veneer Plaster

DIN 4095 Drainage
ASTM WK13764 New Test Method for
    Determining Drainage and Drying
    Characteristics of Drainage Systems
    for Adhered Masonry Veneer Walls
ASTM WK6091 New Test Method for
    Masonry Wall Drainage Systems
ASTM E2273-03 Standard Test Method for
    Determining the Drainage Efficiency of
    Exterior Insulation and Finish Systems
    (EIFS) Clad Wall Assemblies

DIN 18195 Building seals
ASTM C717-09 Standard Terminology of
    Building Seals and Sealants
STP1334   Science and Technology of
    Building Seals, Sealants, Glazing, and
    Waterproofing, vol. 7 (ASTM digital
    library publication)

DIN 18299 General rules for construction work
General rules for construction are regulated
    in local building codes. Please refer to
    the IBC general rules of construction or
    other local codes.

Construction specifications are standardized
    by CSI and its Master Format Division
    List

DIN 18330 Masonry works
C946-91 (1996) e1 Standard Practice for
    construction of dry stacked, surface
    bonded walls
ASTM WK12802 - New Specification for
    Adhered Manufactured Stone Masonry
    Veneer (AMSMV) Units

ACI 530-08 Building Code Requirements & Specification for Masonry Structures and Related Commentaries

Technical contracts are not regulated in the United States. Billing depends on the type of contract. Unit pricing is not commonly used and not standarized.

DIN 18,332 Stone masonry works
ASTM publication: STP1496 Masonry
ASTM committee C18 on Dimension Stone
ASTM C1496-09 Standard Guide for Assessment and Maintenance of Exterior Dimension Stone Masonry Walls and Facades

DIN 18333 Concrete masonry units
ASTM C90 - 09 Standard Specification for Loadbearing Concrete Masonry Units
ASTM C129 - 06 Standard Specification for Nonloadbearing Concrete Masonry Units
ASTM C55 Specification for Concrete BrickASTM C1364 - 07 Standard Specification for Architectural Cast Stone

DIN 18350 Plaster and stucco works
See links at DIN 1964

DIN 18550 Plasters
C109/C109M Test Method for Compressive Strength of Hydraulic Cement Mortars (using 2-in. or 50-mm Cube Specimens)
C305 Practice for Mechanical Mixing of Hydraulic Cement Pastes and Mortars of Plastic Consistency
C511 Specification for Mixing Rooms, Moist Cabinets, Moist Rooms, and Water Storage Tanks Used in the Testing of Hydraulic Cements and Concretes
C778 Specification for Sand

DIN 18550 Masonry, determination of bearing capability of walls and pillars
ASTM C90-09 Standard Specification for Load-Bearing Concrete Masonry Units
ASTM C34 Standard Specification for Structural Clay Load-Bearing Wall Tile
ASTM C145-85 Specification for Solid Load-Bearing Concrete Masonry Units (withdrawn 1990)

DIN 18,951 Adobe structures (eliminated without substitution in 1971)
ASTM E2392-05 Standard Guide for Design of Earthen Wall Building Systems

Notes:
The Masonry Standards Joint Committee's (MSJC) 2008 Building Code Requirements and Specification for Masonry Structures (TMS 402/ACI 530/ASCE 5 and TMS 602/ACI 530.1/ASCE 6) and Commentaries is the newest edition of the national masonry design code and minimum specification and includes numerous changes and enhancements including provisions on self-consolidating grout, reformatted and clearer seismic design requirements, revised anchor bolt capacity equations, and defined inspection frequencies of key aspects of masonry construction. The new edition features "bleed tabs," revision bars, deletion arrows, and movement boxes so that users of the 2005 MJSC will be able to quickly identify sections that have been substantively modified.

Further Reading

Blaser, Werner, Eduardo Souto de Moura, and Jackques Herzog. *Eduardo Souto de Moura: Stein Element Stone* (Basel, Berlin, Boston 2003).
Garner, Lawrence. *Dry Stone Walls* (London, 2005).
Goldsworthy, Andy, and Jerry L. Thompson. *Wall.* (London 1994).
Goldsworthy, Andy. Stone (New York, 1990).
Hayward, Gordon. Stone in the Garden (New York, 2002).
Kapfinger, Otto, and Martin Rauch. *Rammed Earth/Lehm und Architekture/Terra Cruda* (Basel, Berlin, Boston 2001).
McAfee, Patrick. *Irish Stone Walls—History, Building, Conservation* (Dublin, 2000).

Credits

The authors acknowledge the following individuals and companies responsible for walls illustrated in this book on the pages noted:

7 Design: Pierre Tourre, Serge Sanchis, Dominique Le Fur
15 (right) Design: Topotek 1
25 (right top) Design: Pierre Tourre, Serge Sanchis, Dominique Le Fur
27 Design and construction: Andrew Loudon
36, 37 Design and execution: Ralf Schust
45 (left center) Design and execution: Ralf Schust
45 (left bottom) Design: Elke Zimmermann; execution: Markus Nickel
45 (right) Design: Kahn, Singer and Partners; execution: Roland Stärk
47 (bottom) Design: Gustav Lange
49 (top) Design: Mader, Zimmermann; execution: Markus Nickel
49 (bottom) Design: Sven Hansen
51 Execution: Gilles Arnaudo
52 (middle) Design: Charles Jencks
53 Design: Karl Joseph Schattner
55 (both) Design: Edwin Lutyens
57 (both) Design: Hermann Mattern
58 Design: Ian Hamilton Finlay
59 Design: Ian Hamilton Finlay
60 (both) Design: Andy Goldsworthy
61 Design: Andy Goldsworthy; execution: Steve Allen, Max Nowell, Gordon Wilton, Jason Wilton

62, 63 Design: Eduardo de Miguel Rabones, Aranda Muñoz Criado, Vicente Corell, Farinós
65 (top) Execution: Kai Seydell
65 (bottom) Design: Günter Mader; execution: Kai Seydell Company
66 (right) Design: Wolfgang Preuss
67 (right) Design: Pierre Tourre, Serge Sanchis, Dominique Le Fur
69 (left) Design: Dieter Kienast, Günther Vogt and Partner
69 (right) Design: Axel Lohrer, Ursula Hochrein
69 (left) Design: Dieter Kienast, Gunther Vogt and Partner
71 (all) Design: Hans Luz
73 Design: Henning Larsen
74 Design: Günter Mader; execution: Günter Heidt, Ivo Svalina
75 (bottom) Design: Günter Mader, Elke Zimmermann; execution: Georg Weissmüller Company
76, 77 Design: Alain Provost
79 Design: Enric Miralles, Benedetta Tagliabue
80 (bottom) Design: Gilles Vexlard, Laurence Vacherot
81 Design: Gilles Clément, Patrick Berger, Alain Provost, Jean-Paul Viguier, Jean-François Jodry
83 (top) Design: Weber and Sauer
85 Design: Günter Mader; execution: Baum and Park

86, 87 Design: Bernard Huet, Madeleine Ferrand, Jean-Pierre Feugas, Bernard Leroy, Ian Le Caisne, Philippe Raguin
91 (top) Design: Bernard Huet, Madeleine Ferrand, Jean-Pierre Feugas, Bernard Leroy, Ian Le Caisne, Philippe Raguin
91 (bottom) Design: Günter Mader, Elke Zimmermann; execution: Ralf Klischke
92 (both) Design: Silvia Glassler, Udo Dagenbach
93 (top) Design: Jørgen Bo, Vilhelm Wohlert
95 (left) Design: Bernard Huet
95 (right) Design: Regine Keller, Franz Damm
97, Design: Ian Hamilton Finlay
98 (right) Design: Heinz Mohl
99 Design: Kienast, Vogt and Partner
100, 101 Design: Gilles Vexlard, Laurence Vacherot
103 (top) Design: Günter Mader, Elke Zimmermann; execution: Andreas Mokesch Company
108 (both) Design: Weber and Sauer
109 Design: François Brun, Michel Pena
113 Design: Christoph Mann
114, 115 Design: Enric Miralles, Benedetta Tagliabue
117 (top) Design: Karl Bauer

119 Design: Dietmar Herz; execution: Karl Reif
120 Design: Olafur Eliasson
121 (bottom) Design: Enric Miralles, Benedetta Tagliabue
122, 123 Design and execution: Martin Rauch
125 Design and execution: Martin Rauch
127 Design and execution: Martin Rauch
128, 129 Design: Karl Bauer; execution: Jörg Biegert
131 (top) Design: Karl Bauer; execution: Jörg Biegert
131 (bottom) Design and execution: Christoph Ryf

Photo Credits

Photos are by the authors except:
10 (middle and right), 18 Wolfgang Baier, Husum
17 (right middle) Vivian and Erhard Veit, Ebersberg
49 (bottom), 99 Wolfram Müller, Karlsruhe
61 Jerry L. Thompson, New York (from Andy Goldsworthy, *Walls)*
70 (left) Hans Luz, Stuttgart
98 (right) Klaus Kinold, Munich
120 Helmut Claus, Cologne
131 (bottom) Tjards Wendebourg, Stuttgart
133 Michael Lüder, Potsdam